THE DARK NIGHT IS OUR ONLY LIGHT

A Study of the Book of the Dark Night by John of the Cross

Leonard Doohan

ISBN: 978-0991006717
ISBN: 0991006712

ABBREVIATIONS OF THE WORKS

A = Ascent of Mount Carmel
N = Dark Night
C= Spiritual Canticle
F = Living Flame
P = Poetry
S = Sayings of Light and Love
Pr = Precautions
L = Letters

The Author

Dr. Leonard Doohan is Professor Emeritus at Gonzaga University where he was a professor of religious studies for 27 years and Dean of the Graduate School for 13 years. He has written 18 books and 160 articles and has given over 350 workshops throughout the US, Canada, Europe, Australia, New Zealand, and the Far East. Leonard's recent books include *Spiritual Leadership: the Quest for Integrity*, published by Paulist Press in 2007, *Enjoying Retirement: Living Life to the Fullest*, published by Paulist Press in 2010, *Courageous Hope: The Call of Leadership*, published by Paulist Press in 2011, and The *One Thing Necessary: The Transforming Power of Christian Love*, published by ACTA Publications in 2012.

Dr. Doohan has given courses and workshops on John of the Cross all over the world and his published tapes and cds have been used throughout the English speaking countries. Leonard's first book on John of the Cross, *The Contemporary Challenge of John of the Cross*, was published in 1995.

This current book is the second in a new series that explores the major works of John of the Cross for the non-specialist, presenting all the needed background to appreciate this wonderful spiritual writer.

Other books on John of the Cross by Leonard Doohan.

The Contemporary Challenge of John of the Cross
(ICS Publications)

John of the Cross: Your spiritual guide

The Dark Night is Our Only Light: A study of the
book of the *Dark Night* by John of the Cross

The Spiritual Canticle: The Encounter of Two Lovers.
An introduction to the book of the *Spiritual
Canticle* by John of the Cross

The Living Flame of Love

A Year with St. John of the Cross: 365 Daily Readings
and reflections

Table of contents

IN THE FOOTSTEPS OF JOHN OF THE CROSS

The year I finished the manuscript for this book, my wife and I decided to visit the places in Castile connected with the life of John of the Cross. On a previous occasion, after finishing my first book on John, *The Contemporary Challenge of John of the Cross*, we had visited many of the places frequented by John in the south of Spain, particularly in Andalusia. We were excited about our new trip; I had been to Castile on a previous occasion when I taught English one summer to a group of students in Logroño, and then took the opportunity to move south to Avila, Segovia, and some of the surrounding places. My wife and I decided to drive from Italy where we lived at the time, and we ended up driving about 3500 miles, over a period of eighteen days. We drove through varied and wonderful country in Spain— mountains, valleys, badlands, and Montana like areas, fertile farming areas, orchards. We had left Manresa and decided to stop at El Pilar in Zaragoza, a major Marian shrine—what a wonderful place, as was the beautiful San Seo. We arrived in Segovia from Soria on April 22nd. We had stopped in Ciudad de Osma with its wonderful cathedral, public areas, and walking places. Then we moved on to Segovia with its magnificent buildings. As we approached the city, the weather was beautiful and Segovia was at its best, exciting, wonderful, and truly magnificent. Our hotel was just outside the city, but we went in immediately, and like all visitors to Segovia were awestruck at its Roman aqueduct—a truly brilliant work of human creativity. Then we walked through the main streets, focusing on the places that existed in John's time, trying to think how he felt surrounded by such beauty and wealth—the Cathedral, churches, plazas, and buildings of wealthy families and nobility.

The Cathedral of Segovia was destroyed in 1521 during the Comuneros War and the new one constructed under the inspiration of Charles V and dedicated to the Assumption of Mary and to St Frutos, the patron of Segovia. The work began in June 1525, seventeen years before John's birth, and it was not completed until many years after his death. John would have seen the early progress of what became the last great Gothic Cathedral in Spain. From the Cathedral it is a short and easy walk to the great Alcazar of Segovia, dating back to the twelfth century. This magnificent castle looks like something you would see in a children's book, and in fact was one of several that Walt Disney visited as the basis for his castle in Disneyland. This was one of the favorite residences of the monarchs of Castile, and it was from this place that Isabella the Catholic left to be proclaimed Queen in the main square of Segovia in 1474. From the walls of this splendid palace and fortress we could look down on the river Eresma in the valley below and immediately see the Monastery of Discalced Carmelites where John had been prior. In the late afternoon we made our first visit to John's former community and spent time in reflection at his tomb. Since we live near Assisi when in Italy and are used to endless crowds visiting the tomb of St. Francis, it is so different to visit in silence this powerful transformer of spiritual life. It was a simple but wonderful space. We also saw the tomb of Doña Ana of Peñalosa, one of John's disciples and the person to whom he dedicated both the poem and commentary, the *Living Flame of Love.*

The next day we returned to Segovia, stopping first at the church of San Lorenzo, built in the twelfth to the thirteenth centuries and known to John. We then went on to the splendid fifteenth century monastery of Santa Maria del Parral and the community of Hieronymite monks. Not far from the monastery we entered the Church of the True Cross, originally constructed by the Templars in 1208, it is now under the patronage of the Knights of Malta. We passed the Carmelite Monastery and moved on to the sanctuary of Nuestra Señora de la Fuencisla, built in the sixteenth century on an original shrine of the thirteenth century, known to John, to honor the patron of the city and surrounding lands. We then returned to spend time at John's tomb and reflect on some of the central reasons for our visit. After lunch in the old Jewish quarter we wandered around the city again visiting some of the churches that John must have known. Later that evening we returned to view John's monastery from the city walls and then to go outside the monastery to look up at the illuminated Alcazar, truly picturesque and magnificent. You feel a different spirit in this city, reflective, artistic, and historical.

The next day we left Segovia taking the road to Arévalo, which once again passed John's monastery. John's mother Catalina, moved the family to Arévalo in search of work around 1548, and John lived there for three to four years when he was just nine to twelve years old. We visited many of the historical buildings from his days there and had opportunity to speak with the local historian of Arévalo who felt Arévalo had very little influence on John since he was there for only a short time and was so young. He suggested that the section of the town called San Pedro was probably where Catalina's family lived and when we got there we saw several nine year old boys playing in the little square where the bus now stops.

After a picnic lunch we went on to what was to be one of the highlights of our trip, a visit to Medina del Campo.

While I had visited many places connected with John, I had never been here and always wanted to do so; John lived here from 1551-64, the longest time he spent in any place. The young man in the tourist office knew all the places linked to John but recommended that we go straight away to the Carmelite monastery; the current one still containing some of the original monastery of Santa Ana. It turned out to be a great suggestion, since there we met Fr. Juan Jésus who was actually having his lunch when we arrived. When we apologized for interrupting him he said that for him priority must always go to people and their needs, and he could eat lunch later. He took us everywhere and seemed to be able to open doors literally and figuratively all over the city. We first went to the chapel where John of the Cross celebrated his first Mass with his family in the summer of 1567. The chapel was built on the site where the monastery of Santa Ana stood. Part of the original building is now a bar and the chapel is owned by a private family who does not want to spend resources maintaining it and will not let anyone else do it either. It contains two large paintings showing John receiving the habit of the Carmelites in 1563. A year later he would also make his first profession in this monastery. Fortunately they do allow the Carmelites to open it for visitors. We walked around the town, saw where the Jesuit college that John attended used to stand, the little well where tradition suggests John was saved by the Madonna. We then arrived at the Carmelite monastery, the second foundation of Mother Teresa of Avila, and we were taken to the room where Teresa met John of the Cross in 1567 and interviewed him regarding the possibility of him leading the reform of the male branch of Carmel. This is an enclosed community of nuns and we could see where John sat, speaking to Teresa through the grill. Since Fr. Juan Jésus knew that my wife and I both wanted to see the tomb of John's mother, Catalina, which was inside the enclosure and therefore off limits to visitors, he spoke with the Mother Superior who kindly opened the enclosure to allow us to go inside. This was very unusual and quite a privilege, and the noisy opening of bars, keys, and enormous wooden doors gave emphasis to the unusual nature of the visit. My wife has never been inside a monastery enclosure, and I have on just three previous occasions for which I needed the permission of the local Bishop. This gave us a chance to see Catalina's tomb and then to also see the room from Teresa's side where she met John of the Cross. Having spent a pleasant conversation with the Mother Superior and one of the nuns, we left, grateful for their kindnesses. Just a short distance down the street was the Augustinian convent of St Mary Magdalen where John used to work in the sacristy and assist at Mass when he was a boarder at Plague Hospital on the opposite side of the street, now private residences. Unfortunately the monastery was closed since the nuns were singing office. Yet again, a few words from Fr. Juan Jésus and the doors opened and in we went to see a place, so well preserved—almost as it was—and that spoke so well of John's time here as a young boy. As we walked back to the car to say our farewell and express our gratitude to our new friend, Fr Juan Jésus, we passed a private home and bar which used to be the Carmelite monastery prior to the confiscation of religious properties by Juan Alvarez Mendizábal in 1835-37.

Having spent the night in Tordesillas we went on to Salamanca the following day. A magnificent University city, we parked our car on the opposite side of the bridge that led to the Carmen de Abajo, the College of San Andrés, where John stayed as a student while he attended classes in the University of Salamanca. We took the same path he did up to the University, passing the wonderful Dominican Church of San Esteban. Walking around the corridors and into the very classrooms where John studied was both interesting and exciting, especially seeing the old classroom of Luis de León. Salamanca was beautiful, the Cathedral magnificent, the Plaza Major just delightful, the streets and buildings, many of which existed in John's time here, gave a feel for what it must have been like when he lived here in 1564-68.

Our destination was now Avila, but we had two more stops to make on our way there. The first was Alba de Tormes where Teresa died in 1582 and where she is now buried. John met Teresa here in 1571. It looks as if there are plans for a larger basilica in Alba de Tormes which would be a more appropriate center for pilgrims. We then traveled to Fontiveros where John was born. Fontiveros is still a quiet place, but one can see the churches that Catalina must have known and then see the little church built over the birth home of John—he was born here around 1542. The parish church where John was baptized also contains the tombs of his father, Gonzalo de Yepres and his brother, Luis. We arrived in Avila in the early afternoon. Avila is an extraordinary place, certainly one of the most wonderful walled cities of Europe, perfectly preserved. We entered through one of the gates and walked toward the great market place and then on to the Cathedral, considered Spain's first Gothic cathedral. Built around the middle of the twelfth century, it seems partly church and partly fortress and is even built into the city walls so that the apse forms part of the city's fortifications. We walked around amidst the beautiful palaces and left the walled city by the Alcazar gate with its interesting statue to St Teresa and into the Plaza de Santa Teresa, passed the Church of St Peter and moved on to St. Joseph's, Teresa's first foundation of the reform (1563). Generally closed, there was a group being guided around the Church and we were able to slip in and see a little of the Church and museum. Returning to the walled city we stood on the walls above the Paseo del Rastro and looked down on the Monastery of Our Lady of Grace where Teresa as a young woman had been a boarder with the Augustinian nuns. After dinner we drove around the whole city to see the walls illuminated. It had been a very full day.

We started the next day at the monastery of the Incarnation where Teresa had been a novice in 1536 and had been elected prioress in 1571 and then chosen John of the Cross as the community's confessor. As we arrived a nun from a nearby convent who looks after the Church for the Carmelite nuns who are within the enclosure was just leaving and locking up the Church. When I explained my interest in Teresa and John, the fact I have taught courses on their writings for over thirty-five years, and had just finished a book on the *Dark Night*, she opened up every place she could and showed us the Church, Teresa's cell, John's confessional, the parlor where they held discussions, and the grill through which they communicated. John was here from 1572 until 1577 and drew his famous sketch of the crucifixion here, and it was from here that he was taken prisoner, led to Avila and then on to Toledo. I had been to the Incarnation once before and attended Mass here, but now the large grill had been closed off to keep out the cold of the large church. We thanked the sister who with a small community lived in the courtyard of the Incarnation and we returned to the city and could look back from the walls to the Incarnation below. It was said that when Teresa was made prioress the noise of opponents blocking her entrance could be heard from the city walls! We crossed the city passing several palaces from Teresa's time and arrived at the church built over the original home of Teresa which still contains some of the rooms and a little garden. After lunch, we went back to our hotel in the industrial area of Avila and had a short rest. We had already travelled over two thousand miles and at times it seemed we had walked much of it! In the afternoon, we visited the churches of St Vincent, St Andrew, St John of the Cross, and St Francis, all just outside the city walls, and all dating back to Teresa and John's time. In the evening we drove round the illuminated walls one more time, for the next day we began our journey home after a memorable time in Castile. The only place we had not found was Duruelo, even though people told us it was easy to find. Just driving around was interesting, and passing places with names like Salcedo and Pedraza brought back memories of John's life even if these were not the specific places, for several places often have the same name.

Journeying in the footsteps of John of the Cross was a wonderful experience. Visiting the places where he lived and ministered helped us gain perspective on his history, life, and values. As we read his works today, we can picture where he was, what he could see when he wrote, and some of the circumstances that influenced his writings. Journeying with John of the Cross is always exciting and enriching.

Introduction

The book of the *Dark Night* is one of the greatest works of spirituality ever written. It has had enormous influence in the development of our understanding of the spiritual life. It is essential reading for anyone involved in spiritual direction. Moreover, it is foundational for our understanding of God, an individual's spiritual journey, active ascetical training, contemplation, and the goal and purpose of life. It was written by John of the Cross while he was in Granada, around 1582-85, and starts as a commentary on a poem of the same title composed by John around 1579-81, while he was confessor to the nuns in Beas. The book complements the *Ascent of Mount Carmel*, written by John sometime between 1581-85, while he was in El Calvario, Baeza, and Granada. John wrote the poem in light of his experience in the Carmelite monastery prison in Toledo and probably within a year of that terrible experience. The book on the *Dark Night*, as well as the *Ascent* was written over an extended period of time with many interruptions. We have no original versions of John's writings, but we have more copies of the *Dark Night* than any other work of his. Although the *Dark Night* is closely linked to the *Ascent* and can even be considered as Book IV of the latter, it always appears as a separate manuscript.

This short book presents an introduction to the *Dark Night* for anyone who wants to respond to the call and challenge of God to pursue a life that leads to union in love. It is not written for scholars but for an audience similar to the one John had in mind when he wrote this astonishing book on the dark night. John wrote for religious, clergy, and laity who were already dedicated to the pursuit of a God-centered life and had reached a point where their hearts were open to the further challenges of God that come in contemplation. John's *Dark Night* passes beyond what dedicated individuals strive to do on their own initiative, with their own plans, in light of their own goals. The *Dark Night* reminds us that all this is good, but only a preparation. What really matters in the spiritual life is not what we do but what God does in us. So, the *Dark Night* is a major transition in spiritual life, an opening of our minds, hearts, and memories to the transformation that God brings to those individuals who yearn for fullness of life.

This book reminds us of the dark nights of John's own life, the hard experiences that influenced his work. It presents key aids that can help us understand the *Dark Night* and an exposition of the *Dark Night*. Following an abbreviated form of John's book, it considers some of the key spiritual challenges contained in the *Dark Night*. Then it looks at contemporary experiences of the dark night. Finally, it considers questions that often arise for interested readers of the *Dark Night*. The *Dark Night* is a book about light, guidance, and illumination. May this short introduction help readers understand a little more John's great work, and so enable them to be more open to a life of union with God in love.

CHAPTER ONE
JOHN OF THE CROSS AND THE DARK NIGHTS OF HIS OWN LIFE

John of the Cross lived from 1542 until 1591. He had very clear goals for what he wanted to achieve in life, namely the ultimate state of human, Christian maturity available to any man or woman. He pursued his goal no matter the situations he encountered, no matter the pain and sacrifice he needed to endure. He single-mindedly and single-heartedly sought to redirect the whole of his life to attain union with God in love, and his life evidenced a commitment to always choose what was the most loving thing to do. From early childhood through years of education and spiritual formation he prepared himself, and let God prepare him, to attain the quality of life he sought. He accepted hardship and relentlessly pursued a life of union with God. Sacrifice quickly became a part of his life, but so too did persecution and darkness. Even when he chose to give himself to the challenges of reform and a return to the rigors of primitive observance, he experienced misunderstanding, pain, suffering, persecution, and abandonment, both from those who opposed him and from those who claimed to be with him. His life was full of dark night experiences, and he becomes a model for us in approaching the dark nights of our own lives.

Early Years—Born Into Hardship

John of Yepes, the future John of the Cross, was born in 1542 in Fontiveros, then a town of about 5,000 inhabitants, situated twenty four miles northwest of Avila, on the Castilian plateau. John was the third child of Gonzalo de Yepes and Catalina Alvarez, the former from a family of wealthy silk merchants in Toledo but also an orphan, the latter a poor orphaned girl. When his family saw that Gonzalo married below his status, choosing his love for Catalina instead of family wealth, they disowned and disinherited him and showed ongoing abhorrence for Catalina. Gonzalo's family included an inquisitor and three canons—all interpreting religion with severity and unyielding stubbornness. However, in hardship, poverty, malnutrition, and sickness, Gonzalo and Catalina built their life on love and shared the wealth of their goodness with all they encountered. Gonzalo lost his position as merchant-manager for his wealthy family and learned from Catalina how to weave wool and silk. John was born into this life where love had priority over material goods and sharing over accumulation. He experienced the value of poverty and hardship and appreciated how rejection can purify and lead to wholeness.

Not long after John's birth, Gonzalo died after a prolonged, painful illness, leaving his young widow, Catalina, without means to bring up her three sons; Francisco, Luis (who soon died, apparently of malnutrition), and the youngest, John, who was no more than a few years old. Around this time, Fontiveros was overwhelmed with famine and drought—the so-called "barren years," when prices for basic necessities skyrocketed, and the family lived in poverty. Catalina decided to make the ninety mile journey to beg help from Gonzalo's brothers, only to face constant rejection from Gonzalo's relatives who refused to aid the struggling family. One of Gonzalo's brothers helped for a while, giving a place to

Francisco, but his wife mistreated Francisco and Catalina took him back to her own home.

Catalina with her family left Fontiveros, her home, friends, family memories, and tombs of her husband and son, and went in search of work and food, settling first in Arévalo for three to four years. While in Arévalo, Catalina arranged a marriage for Francisco to Ana Izquierdo. In their early married life a new pain afflicted the family—seven of eight children died prematurely, the first while they were still in Arévalo. Catalina shared her home with Francisco and his wife,

Later, Catalina and family moved to Medina del Campo, a Castilian town of about 30,000, a favorite of Isabella, the Catholic Monarch, who died here in 1504. This was the family's third and final move, for in Medina they found work and food and immersed themselves in charitable activities for the needy. John lived here for thirteen years, from age nine to twenty-two (1551-64). Around this time, Catalina sent young John to one of Medina's so-called Catechism schools, boarding schools where orphans learned a trade and were fed and clothed by the support of generous benefactors. Later, John moved to Conception Hospital and showed considerable ability and interest in hospital ministry, both in his dedicated and loving service of the patients and in begging for financial support for the hospital's many needs. John also learned excellent administrative skills from Don Alonso Alvarez de Toledo, the gentleman who gave his wealth and life to the service of the hospital. At 17, while continuing his work at the hospital, John began studying at the nearby Jesuit College, where he showed significant success at school work and developed a love for study. Although given little time for school work, John delighted in studying at night, and began to feel at home in the experiences of the night.

During this time, Catalina and her extended family continued to struggle in poverty, but always shared the little they had with others, less fortunate, including abandoned orphans. Catalina had trained Francisco and John well; both were experts in the service of the poor, sick, and needy; and these qualities would remain with John throughout his life. He learned that accumulation of material goods has no real value; whatever you have can become a source of richness. Their move from self-centeredness to other-centeredness became the model for John's own life. Moreover, Catalina and Francisco had the gift of helping people to find satisfaction in giving and responding to the needs of others, a lesson John would never forget. They taught John the importance of simple, honest, dedicated work, purity in relationships and love, and the enriching values of family and friendships.

Reflection points

- *John lived in poverty, deprivation, and constant hardship and learned how one can grow and mature not in spite of these aspects of life, but because of them.*

- *John loved his mother and brothers but also saw how misplaced family values—meaning the preservation of one's blood line and status (like Gonzalo's family sought)—can destroy authentic love.*

- *John quickly experienced that life is a series of exodus. Later he would begin all his major poems with an action word in the first verse—describing stages in our journey to the Promised Land.*

- *In stories about his father's brothers—including an inquisitor and three canons—John saw first hand how legalistic religion can lead one away from God and the values of authentic love.*

- *John apprenticed as a carpenter, painter, tailor, and sculptor; he ministered in the hospitals; and he immersed himself in study. He discovered no situation, no ministry, no institution, no amount of study can of themselves lead one to God. This was a personal decision he had to face.*

Carmel before the Reform—Seeking God

John was increasingly respected by the people of Medina and was offered employment opportunities and invited to join religious orders. Several of these opportunities could have given John a benefice that would have sustained him and the family for years to come. John's choices lay elsewhere. One day in 1563, unknown to those interested in his future, John entered the Carmelite monastery where he would be known as Brother John of St. Matthias. He seems to have been attracted by the Carmelites' dedication to prayer and their Marian piety. After what seems to have been a happy novitiate year, John was professed and soon obtained permission to observe what was thought to be the primitive rule of the order.[1]

In 1564, John arrived in the great university city of Salamanca, where he took up residence at the college of San Andrés, a Carmelite house of studies. John had already developed a good knowledge of the humanities and was sent to further his studies especially in philosophy and theology. Salamanca was an extraordinary city of which John had never seen the likes, and when he arrived it was at its peak in splendor, art, architecture, and outstanding university life. Over 6000 students attended the university; John was there for four years (1564-68) and studied under some of the outstanding scholars of the day, including Luis de León. John was an excellent student and his later writings demonstrate his brilliant grasp of philosophy, theology, and Scripture.

Although in these years at Salamanca John learned much about God, he also appreciated that intellectual knowledge, even at the highest levels, does not necessarily bring one closer to God or help one to experience God. So, John passed through a creative crisis regarding the essential role of contemplation in his life and the pursuit of union with God in love. He found that pain, darkness, and self-questioning can lead to illumination. The university lectures were challenging, given by some of the greatest scholars of the day, and life at San Andrés was one of cultivated recollection and a contemplative approach to one's studies. Salamanca offered John plenty of occasions to integrate studies and spirituality, and by the time John left Salamanca he was well versed in matters of prayer, spirituality, contemplation, and major ascetical writings—most of which he would have had to study on his own. In Salamanca John learned to integrate speculative theology and mystical theology, aware that the mystical always predominates. He continued to live by the primitive rule of the order and was well known for his prolonged prayer and penances. John appreciated that studies, piety, cultivated religious environments, even stricter religious disciplines did not guarantee closer union with God. Certainly, John may well have been a little put off by the emphasis on careerism among the students of Salamanca, but he seemed happy in his chosen life, and yet basically he yearned for something more.

At the end of his third year of theology, John went to Medina del Campo to celebrate his first Mass with his family. In the late summer of 1567, he met Mother Teresa of Avila, to whom John had been recommended as a possible leader in the reform of the friars. Teresa was 52 at the time and John was just 25. When they first met, Teresa was already a woman of spiritual stature in Castile, and she had already written the second version of her *Autobiography* in 1565 and the *Way of Perfection* in 1566. John told Teresa that he was considering transferring to the Carthusians, but she insisted that his desires for contemplation, solitude, and penance could be fulfilled in her reformed Carmel. John never despised the good he had, but he always strove for more—for union with God.

Reflection points

- *When John lived in Salamanca, it was a place where careers developed; students knew how to learn the litmus tests that would gain them promotion. John could have played the games of the day, but he knew this approach to religion never leads to God.*

- *Anyone who reads John of the Cross' great works knows that he is not anti-intellectual. Rather his studies gave him foundations, background, system, and means of articulation—and he was outstanding in using his studies. But they are not an end, for he quickly learned that the intellect must be purified by faith.*

- *In Salamanca, John struggled with the direction of his own life; he experienced questions concerning his vocation, pain, and darkness, and he had an early awareness of how these can lead to illumination.*

- *John never despised the good he had experienced but strove for something more—this would become a constant feature of his life.*

- *Salamanca was known for the splendor and power of the Church where future leaders were trained. John shows us how the Church is built up from the grassroots in the dedication of individuals and the teaching authority of their sanctity.*

The Early Reform – A Time to Welcome Sacrifice

In the summer of 1568, Teresa visited Medina del Campo and met again with John and his first companion in the reform, Antonio de Heredia. Teresa had assigned tasks to each of them the previous year to prepare for the setting up of the friars' first house of the reform at Duruelo. Antonio had arranged for the transfer of his responsibilities as prior and also found some basic necessities for the monastery in Duruelo. John had finished his studies and visited Francisco de Salcedo, one of Teresa's good friends and early advisors, to receive counsel from him. Teresa herself found the building in Duruelo, a rather dilapidated place, but John and Antonio welcomed the call to live there. In addition to material and organizational preparations, Teresa was also very concerned with the spiritual formation of the first friars of the reform, especially John on whom she placed her hopes for the renewal she sought. In view of this, Teresa took John with her on her travels, especially to Valladolid where she was establishing a new foundation. This gave her ample opportunity to teach John about her own vision for the reform, but maybe Teresa unexpectedly found she was also learning from her new disciple, even sharing with him some of the confidences of her inner spirit. Both developed trust in dealing with the other, both were strong willed personalities, and Teresa acknowledged disagreements over business and organizational matters.

Duruelo was an out of the way place, nothing more than a few scattered buildings, but a place of silence, solitude, and humility. John and his traveling companion, a stonemason, began to put their monastery into livable conditions, cleaning it and setting up chapel, choir, and cells. More importantly, they soon organized their common life in times of work, prayer, and ministry in the local area. They lived simply, avoiding the gifts of food from generous neighbors, preferring to maintain their lives of penance.

The monastery was so simple and evocative of a spirit of penance that even Teresa when she later visited was amazed, and went so far as to ask the friars not to be so rigorous in their penitential practices. The friars lived in total dedication in their small, uncomfortable, poorly furnished hovel, going out only for their ministry of preaching and instruction for the local people, who gained enormous respect for the friars.

On November 28th 1568, the provincial celebrated the official foundation of the monastery at Duruelo, and John took the vows of the reform, together with Antonio de Jesus. John then took as his new name, John of the Cross. This first community of the reform was an experimental community within the larger Carmelite order. For John it was the realization of his dreams for a more rigorous and contemplatively focused life. Duruelo offered penance, sacrifice, simplicity, solitude and community, and a chance to focus on the wholehearted pursuit of the love of God. From the beginning, the friars also gave themselves to the needs or the people around them.

As new members came to join the community, the monastery at Duruelo became too small, no matter how many modifications the friars made. Several benefactors offered alternatives, and in June of 1570 the community moved to Mancera de Abajo. Around this time, John went to Pastrana, the second house of the reform. Teresa started this community when she responded to a request from two hermits to admit them into the community, following a recommendation of the Council of Trent. When John arrived, this community had about 15 friars, and John took on the task of novice master—a position he held in Mancera de Abajo, setting up a general program of formation. He stayed only a short time and then returned to his own monastery. Life continued in Mancera de Abajo, John met Teresa again on her way to Alba de Tormes in Salamanca; she was accompanied by a novice, Ann of Jesus, to whom John would later dedicate the *Spiritual Canticle*.

In April 1571, John was chosen as rector of the Discalced Carmelite house of studies in Alcalá de Henares—a university city second only to Salamanca, where his prime responsibility was the students' spiritual growth. Some accused John of encouraging excessive mortification, but the Dominican apostolic commissioner, called to resolve the issue, was strong in his support of John and the quality of formation he was giving. When, a short time later, John was asked to intervene in a dispute between frustrated novices in

Pastrana and the excessive practices required by their novice master, John, stressing that penance was a means and not the end of spiritual training, urged moderation, and was supported by both Teresa and the great theologian, Domingo Bañez.

Thus, the reform began in simplicity and poverty. Today, practically nothing remains of Duruelo (a simple cross), Mancera (a Calced monastery for nuns), Pastrana (abandoned), and Alcalá (abandoned). But the spirit of love and dedication discovered, taught, and celebrated in these places continues to flourish in the perennial challenge of John of the Cross.

In 1571, Teresa was appointed prioress of the convent of the Incarnation in Avila, where she had spent 27 years before beginning the reform. Teresa had referred to this monastery as "Babylon," and when she arrived for her installation, the doors were barred by disgruntled nuns and their protests could be heard from the walls of the city of Avila, over half a mile away. The first weeks were oppressive for Teresa, who became quite ill. She made the unusual request that John of the Cross be appointed confessor; unusual because the convent of the Incarnation was Calced and John Discalced, they were not part of the reform and he clearly was. Eventually, John became, along with Teresa, one of the two principal spiritual guides of the Incarnation, and by the end of 1572 peace and renewal were coming to the convent. John was in his early thirties, but already a theologian, reformer, novice master, rector, confessor, exorcist, and visionary. The Lord continued to enrich John's mature spiritual life with deeper experiences.

Reflection points

- *John's involvement in the history of the early reform presents us with so many insignificant places and events, and yet like the mustard seed these heralded the great things that were to come about.*

- *John made many choices which were not accumulative of his love for God, but were choice-oriented decisions that created his personality.*
- *From early in the reform John became a spiritual director for so many. When we read his great commentaries they are filled with practical advice based on the many real situations with which he had dealt.*
- *John was known for his many sacrifices and penances. He saw all these as means to the end of the pursuit of the love of God.*
- *John never saw enrichment as accumulation, but as a process of stripping oneself of all, so that the inner life of God's love can be allowed to grow on its own, unhindered by our false values.*

Persecuted By His Enemies

Reform and renewal always have their enemies: the constant power of evil, well-intentioned people who are misinformed or unwilling to change, men and women who gain power from religion and are reluctant to let it go, and those whose reforming zeal masks self-interested motives. Not everyone was enthusiastic about the Teresian Carmelite reform; both Teresa and John had their critics and opponents. During the reform there were not only clashes between the new discalced Carmelites and their parent order, but conflicts among Papal, Imperial, and Carmelite authorities. In 1575 the Carmelite General Chapter was held in Piacenza, Italy. Fr. Rubeo had written twice to Teresa, asking for explanations regarding the reform, but she did not receive the correspondence until June, and her silence was interpreted as rebellion. Decisions were made that were unfavorable to the reform. Since the Discaled had no representatives at the General Chapter they decided to meet in Almodóvar in 1576 to clarify their own position and possibly to send representatives to Rome to lobby for the reform, but this meeting further angered the Calced Carmelites. In June 1577, the Papal Nuncio, Nicolás Ormaneto died and was replaced by Felipe Sega—the former a supporter of the Discalced and the latter a supporter of the Calced and an opponent of the reform. In 1577 the monastery of the Incarnation met to elect a new prioress. The Calced with the support of the authorities wanted to elect Doña Juana de Aguila, but 54 of the 98 nuns insisted on electing Teresa. They were excommunicated and yet insisted on reaffirming their votes, and, when they were offered absolution, they refused unless their claims were recognized. So, with these and similar events, tensions were building up. On December 3-4, 1577, the Incarnation was attacked by armed men, who broke down the door and seized John and his companion, bound them, took them off to the Carmelite monastery and whipped them. On the second day of his imprisonment John slipped past his guard and returned to the Incarnation to destroy documents that could have proved incriminating to members of the reform. John was then recaptured, blindfolded, and taken secretly to Toledo. The journey over the mountains was rough, cold, uncomfortable, and painful, so that even the muleteer and an innkeeper tried to arrange John's escape, though grateful, he refused to cooperate. John arrived at the large monastery of Toledo, leaving behind his simple homes in Duruelo, Pastrana, and his cell at Avila. Toledo was an awesome city, then the capital of Spain. Earlier in the year, possibly having seen the great palaces of the kings, Teresa of Avila had written her *Interior Castle*. The same year, the artist, El Greco, began his work just a street or so away from John's prison.

In December 1577, John was brought before the tribunal of Jerónimo Tostado, the Carmelite General's visitator, who threatened, cajoled, and even tried to bribe John to reject the reform and to submit to the decisions of the Chapter of Piacenza. John refused, confident that the Discalced had been acting under the higher authority of the papal nuncio. For this he was declared a rebel and placed in the official monastery prison. After two months when it became known that John's companion had escaped from his prison in Avila, John was transferred to another cell specially prepared for him. Originally a lavatory for an adjoining room, it was about nine by five feet, with only a tiny window high up on the wall to give light. John's bed was nothing more that a board and two old blankets. Dressed only in his tunic and left only his breviary to read, John was imprisoned for nearly nine months, weak from illness, deprived of the liturgy, suffering from hunger, frostbite in winter, searing heat in summer, and profound abandonment. On Monday, Wednesday, and Friday he was given only bread and water, and on Wednesday every member of the community joined in a communal public lashing of John. He was not allowed to wash and never given a change of clothes in the first six months he was there.

During this time no one among the Discalced knew where John was, in fact neither did Teresa in spite of her efforts to gain the support of Philip II. John's brothers of the reform did very little to find him. Although some friars in the Toledo monastery, especially from the student years in Salamanca, admired him, they were strictly bound to silence and unable to support him. However, after six months, a friar assigned as John's new warden gave him clean clothes and writing material. Once August came, John began planning his escape, convinced this was his only chance of ever leaving alive. His daring escape began when he lowered himself from a window in the corridor outside his cell, having loosened the lock screws in the previous days. He made his way through Toledo by night and hid in the cloister of the Discalced Carmelite nuns' convent, and later transferred to the private quarters of Pedro Gonzalez de Mendoza, administrator of the Hospital of Santa Cruz. From the safety of his room John could see the window through which he had escaped.

Clearly, the treatment John received during his prison experience was cruel and inhumane; nowadays we would call it torture, with its interplay of physical and psychological punishments given with the desire to break him and make him conform. John endured the deprivation, hunger, cold, and abandonment, as well as human degradation, solitary confinement, fear of poisoning, and perverse suggestive voices programmed from the nearby room. He lived in darkness, nakedness, and emptiness, and discovered their beauty. The Toledo cell is the perfect image of readiness for growth—dark, empty, anxious, deprived, suffering—ready to be filled. One of the great gifts of life is to see what others cannot see, to look at something in a way no one else can, and to understand that life has meaning only when interpreted in light of a realm beyond the normal horizons of life. John never criticized his tormentors, but viewed his experiences in light of God's ongoing call to him to dedicate his life in love. Thus, this prison time became a creative period in his life as he wrote some of the most beautiful poetic verses of all time. It also became his own most intense experience of the dark night, although he did not write the poem until some time later, probably during his stay at El Calvario.

Reflection points

- *John lived at a time when the Church evidenced various power blocks, struggling among themselves. Spiritual growth and the pursuit of union with God must develop no matter the situations in the Church.*
- *Religion in every generation has it own ways of punishing those who do not tow the party line. For John, fidelity is primarily to the call of God.*
- *Mystical life does not exclude practical gifts, needs, and responsibilities. John was a business professional, a good organizer, and could even plan his own escape while drawn to God in love.*
- *John lived in darkness, emptiness, nakedness, and overwhelming suffering. He emerged transformed in love and convinced that the dark night is our only guide.*

- *John lived through cruel and inhuman treatment but never became embittered. Pain can purify, darkness can illuminate, aloneness can give appreciation of community, sickness can help one appreciate healing, hunger can focus on what truly satisfies, torture can help emphasize mutual goodness. Love conquers all.*

Trials among His Own

John spent about a month in hospital after his escape and contrary to the urgings of his friends decided to attend a meeting of the Discalced in Almodóvar in October. Two of Don Pedro's men assisted John during his journey, as he remained very weak. From Almodóvar John travelled on to Beas still aided by Don Pedro's servants. At Beas they left him in the care of the nuns in the local monastery. He was still exhausted but shared with the nuns the joy he felt in his sufferings at Toledo. He reached El Calvario, a place he loved, in the countryside, with open spaces, solitude, and lots of light! What a difference from his prison cell in Toledo. At the time, El Calvario was known for austerity beyond even the rule of the Discalced, and John—now superior—led the community to moderation and a greater emphasis on contemplation. John gave himself wholeheartedly to the spiritual guidance of the community of El Calvario and also to the nuns in Beas.

In the spring of 1579, the faculty of the University of Baeza made it known that they wanted a college for Carmelite students, and John responded, opening the house on June 13th and becoming the first rector. Baeza was a city of about 50,000 with a flourishing wool and silk industry. On June 22, 1580, Gregory XIII granted the request of the Discalced to become a separate province, and they held their first provincial chapter in March of the following year, at which John was elected one of the four councilors to the new provincial, Jerónimo Gracián. In November of the same year

Gracián sent John to Avila for discussions with Teresa. It was the first time John had seen Teresa since his imprisonment, and the last time he would see her before her death the following year. Soon afterwards, John was elected prior of Granada.

Tensions developed within the Discalced, between Gracián's emphasis on Teresa's vision of life and ministry and Nicolás Doria's emphasis on austerity and observance. When Doria became provincial he expelled Gracián from the order, a decision John of the Cross opposed. In 1585 John was appointed vicar for Andalusia, and this involved even more travel for him. In fact, in the course of his life, John traveled over 16,000 miles, with all the hardships and discomfort of those days, not to mention natural dangers and banditry. In 1588 John was elected first consultor to Doria and chosen prior of Segovia. John always missed Castile and was very happy to return to take up residence in Segovia, a city richly endowed by Philip II. This was John's third visit to Segovia. The monastery was outside the city and its gardens offered the solitude and reflection John cherished. But this was also a busy time dealing with the business of the order, growing tensions among the brethren, and Doria's request that John restructure and enlarge the monastery as a worthy place for the central administration of the order. It is amazing how John maintains balance between manual work, pressure-filled decisions, spiritual direction, and contemplation in solitude.

In June 1591, John attended another chapter in Madrid. According to one version of events, Fr. Doria's uneasiness about John had been growing in recent months, partly for his support of Teresa's spirit, and because he suspected John disapproved of his extreme measures against Gracián, and partly because he mistakenly thought John was behind a recourse the nuns had made to Rome to free them from Doria's interventions. John, realizing that many chapter members felt intimidated from expressing their true sentiments and were subject to intrigue, asked unsuccessfully for secret voting. He himself spoke out fearlessly in opposition to radical measures against the nuns and Gracián. In the end, whether as a punishment or not, John was left without a position of authority, something he had actually wished. In fact, John had volunteered for Mexico, a proposal unanimously accepted by the chapter. Yet Doria later changed his mind about John, and considered sending him back to Segovia as prior. John paid a visit to Segovia, but even then to those with whom he spoke he seemed fully aware that his end was near.

John set off for Andalusia, thinking he was on his way to Mexico. He stayed first at La Peñuela, where he reworked his commentary on the *Living Flame of Love*. While in La Peñuela John began experiencing high fever and painful swelling in his right leg. During this time Fr. Diego Evangelista, a revengeful, suspicious, and self-centered friar whom John had once reprimanded, began a deplorable process of attempting to disgrace John by insinuating that his interactions with the many nuns he directed had been improper. Unfortunately, Doria never prevented Diego Evangelista, now a member of Doria's inner counsel, in his attempted humiliation of John. This same Diego Evangelista also helped Doria in gathering information against other opponents, notably Gracián.

As John's sickness continued, the monastery's superior wanted him to go to a larger community to receive appropriate care. John had the choice of Baeza where he was well known and loved, or Ubeda where he was little known. He chose the latter. John became ill and was transferred to Ubeda for treatment. There he was humiliated again by yet another vengeful friar who still resented having been corrected by John many years before: Francisco Crisostomo. Informed of John's mistreatment, Fr Antonio, John's first companion in the reform and now provincial of Andalusia, hastened to Ubeda to rectify the treatment of John. After his arrival in Ubeda, John's sickness worsened with abscesses and fever. So-called cures in those days were brutal, but John's patience under suffering was extraordinary. John of the Cross died at midnight on Saturday, December 14th 1591. He was 49 years old, and had given himself to the reform for 23 years.

Reflection points

- *The ordinary pressures of daily life, illness, weariness, quantity of work, travel, can wear one down. John's spiritual growth took place within all the real events of a busy daily life.*
- *John showed a spirit of obedience throughout life. One sacrifice some people must face, as John did, is to speak out against corruption and injustice while maintaining respectful obedience.*
- *There are always places that seem to nourish one's spiritual life more than others. For John, El Calvario could do that. But each of us, like John, must create our own sacred space amidst the clutter of ordinary life.*
- *John was a person of single-minded integrity. While we more frequently think of maintaining integrity in confrontation with an unethical world, people of integrity must sometimes also stand up against people in authority as John did.*
- *Death is the last stage in manifesting the values of life. John's death was a model of union with God in love. There were a lot of ordinary times in John's life, but it is wonderful to see the ordinary overwhelmed with love.*

John—an Inspiration for Our Journey through the Nights[2]

John was under five feet tall, thin from his sacrifice and imprisonment, and oval faced with a little growth of beard and mustache. He wore the rough brown habit of the reform, a coarse white mantle, and sometimes a dark brown skull-cap.

Contemporaries said that, although clearly ascetical, he had a pleasing appearance and was interesting to talk to. He was always in control of himself; peaceful, calm, and quietly joyful. He was simple, straightforward, and shunned all manifestations of authority. Those who knew him said he was polite, delicate and gentle in dealing with others, and could share both their manual work and their recreation. He loved the beauty of nature, and deep friendships were important to him. He was a compassionate person, particularly sensitive to the poor, sick, and suffering. Above all, John was a giant in the spiritual life, drawing teaching of universal value from experience, both his own and others.

John's early life already showed traces of values that were to make up the general direction of his future. He could see, in the example of his parents, what it meant to sacrifice all for the sake of true love. The poverty of his family showed him that mere accumulation of things does not guarantee love and happiness. However, the pain and struggles that came with poverty made John sensitive to deprivation in others and always ready to alleviate it where he could. His family fostered piety, and John treasured such attitudes throughout his life, especially devotion to Mary. Compassionate charity, learned especially in his hospital service, became a permanent feature in his concern for others. At considerable personal sacrifice, John always integrated study into his life, from the early years in Medina del Campo right up to his last years in Andalusia. Deep love for God and for others was the special quality that permeated John's whole life, as it did his message. Poverty, charity, piety, study, authenticity, and deep love formed permanent parts of John's life.

John was a man of destiny. From his early life, when friends had all kinds of plans for him, he had a clear picture of what he wanted from life. He had a sense of vocation—personally called by God. He worked in the hospital, was successful, enjoyed the work, but knew there is more to life than generous, successful ministry. He went to the Jesuit school in Medina, thoroughly enjoyed study, valued it all his life, but recognized that for him there was more to life than education. Entering the Order of Mount Carmel, attracted by its spirit of contemplation and Marian piety, he had a happy novitiate and learned to encounter God in new ways. But this experience too, great as it was, did not satisfy John's yearning for God. He then went to Salamanca for theology, a chance to study about God, but no amount of study alone led him to union with God. He decided to join the Carthusians, but Teresa encouraged him to seek the deeper contemplative union he wanted in her renewed Carmel. By the age of 25, John had learned that ministry, education, religious life, and theology do not automatically insure union with God. Even reforming an institution to facilitate the life one seeks is no guarantee. John sensed an irresistible attraction to God and pursued this goal uncompromisingly and relentlessly. What he had experienced he valued but, without despising previous experiences, he left them aside to continue the search in new ways.

Some people accumulate many small manifestations of love for God. Others make a single-minded, single-hearted choice for love of God, and see everything as secondary to the quest for God's love. Accumulated love rarely implies renunciation; choice-oriented love always does. In choice-oriented love the seeker renounces all that up to the present was viewed as the best means available, renounces without despising previous means, moves forward to the goal of life. Choice-love is creative of one's personality, as is evident in John, who sought God even through the nights, journeying to the union for which he yearned. Accumulated small expressions of love never substitute for choice-oriented love, even though they may help to manifest and maintain it. Choice-oriented love is the clearest indicator of ongoing conversion, while accumulated love can still be shown by someone who refuses to face the need for a total conversion and transformation.

When you read the life of John of the Cross you cannot help but be filled with sadness, joy, peace, and a sense of wonder and awe. Reading his life is exciting. John integrated all the best values from his experience in one great thrust of self-dedication to God. His goal was always clear, never neglected or watered down; he pursued it with the united effort of all his strength, talents, and unified affectivity. His was not a selfish goal of personal growth, for he took others along with him, sharing the vision and the love by which he felt drawn.

John shows us how to live in a struggle-filled post-conciliar Church, since he himself entered Carmel the year the Council of Trent finished its deliberations. He learned to cope with people who resisted the renewal he wanted, with ecclesiastical authorities interested in the power that religion brings, with the spite of some, the envy of others, and dishonest slander of still others. Through all his struggles, he maintained true priorities and proved that contemplative union is possible under any circumstances. John's life was one long night. Sometimes he was directly and actively involved in the purifications of the night; the deprivations of Duruelo, the horrors of Toledo, the sacrifices of his travels. He even readied himself for the coming of the night, opening himself to the hardships of life, readying himself for contemplation, letting go and letting be, living peacefully in a world of tension, accepting betrayal by his own. At other times he welcomed the transforming effects of a night experience; cherishing silence and welcoming divine interventions, immersing himself in gratitude to God, humbly perceiving his own sin, lovingly accepting suffering for love, peacefully accepting attempts to destroy him, losing all religious supports in prison. Then, he also welcomed the transforming effects of a night over which he had no control, especially the complete abandonment in the prison of Toledo and his total openness and receptivity to the challenge of grace. John's night was at times a dark night, at times a guiding night, certainly a transforming night, and in the end a night more lovely than the dawn. A man of wisdom, John journeyed to the mountain top and teaches us how to get there: the dark night is our only guide.

CHAPTER TWO
INFLUENCES ON JOHN'S WRITING OF THE DARK NIGHT

John loved to study, and he read extensively. He knew philosophy and theology very well and had an outstanding knowledge of Scripture which he used according to the normal practice of this period. He also read poetry and used both concepts and ideas from influential poets of his day. However, all these influences are indirect, and John's work is completely original. Nevertheless, he was influenced by the environment in which he lived, especially Castile and Andalusia, and by the times in which he lived. It was a golden age for Spain, a time of post-conciliar renewal in the Church, but also a time of maintaining orthodoxy and of dealing with the impositions of the Inquisition. John was also influenced by the experiences of his ministry with the poor, sick, and needy, with his work among the nuns and friars of the reform, and with his outreach to many laity from all walks of life. Finally, John was also influenced by reliving his spiritual experiences in his poetry, by his reflections in preparation for his writings, and by the many people for whom he was spiritual director. His life was a rich combination of influences, all coming together to help him give us his greatest works.

The Environment in Which John Lived

Spain and Castile. At the time of John of the Cross, Spain was not the united country it is today. True, the larger parts of Spain had been united by the marriage of Isabella of Castile and Ferdinand of Aragon in 1469, who had then gone on to re-conquer the south and especially Granada from the Moors in 1481-1492, earning for themselves the title "Catholic Monarchs." While establishing a unity not previously seen, each part of Spain remained independent and viewed others as foreigners. The Catholic Monarchs had also expanded Spain's powerful empire in the New World (1492), including Mexico (1519), and Peru (1531-33). Religious unity was seen as part of political unity and the Inquisition was authorized in 1478 to enforce religious uniformity. Later, all residents of Spain were forced to be Christians, including the Moors of Granada (Moriscos) and Jews throughout the nation. As a result of these forced conversions, in 1568 a savage rebellion broke out between the Christians and Moriscos of Andalusia.

In 1516 Charles I succeeded his grandfather, Ferdinand, and in 1519 became Charles V, Holy Roman emperor, whose lands included Spain, Netherlands, Austria, Southern Germany, and Italy. In 1556 Philip II became king of Spain and the Spanish territories oversees. He moved his court from Toledo to Madrid in 1560. John of the Cross (1542-1591) lived during the time of Philip II (1556-1598), the golden age of Spain and a time of imperial expansion but also of great development in art, literature, architecture, social, political, and religious life. Spain's empire extended around the world, universities increased in number and importance, many of Europe's greatest scholars and artists were Spanish, and religious renewal was widespread.

John spent the first 36 years of his life in Castile, with the exception of his four years in Salamanca, León. Castile was the heart of Spain, a region of great wealth but also of poverty, as the region was drained to support the nation's involvement in wars. Castile was also a place of great beauty and contrasts. Castile was "a landscape of savage boulders and treeless plain, reaching away to where the mountains stood, sharp as a flint edge, upon the skyline. The winter was bitter, the summer heat without mercy. The light was hard, shadows black and clear-cut. There were no half tones, no softness. It was the landscape that helped to mold a people to whom life presented itself in extremes. Todo o nada. All or nothing. Heat or cold, Light or darkness. Truth or falsehood. God or the devil."[3]

Toledo. John arrived in Toledo in December 1577 and would spend nine months in the prison there. Toledo was a beautiful city, until recently the nation's capital. It stands on a hill, with the river Tagus flowing around it; it gives the impression of openness to the sky, an architectural masterpiece where the renaissance of the north meets the Moorish influences of the south; the Mudeja reminds travelers that the Moors conquered Toledo as far back as the tenth century. The Carmelite monastery was quite close to Toledo's great castle and at the same time not far from the river Tagus. John's tiny cell had only a small slit for a window. Here John suffered the deepest darkness of spirit, doubt, and uncertainty, even though of his trials he later wrote, "Well and good if all things change, Lord God, provided we are rooted in you" (S. 34). Here John was immersed in darkness and could hear only the rhythmic flow of the river. Here he wrote "By the streams of Babylon" and also the poem "For I know well the spring that flows and runs, although it is night." He wrote the latter around the feast of Corpus Christi—a wonderful expression of Trinitarian theology and spirituality that culminates with the gift of the Eucharist. Possibly around Christmas, John wrote the nine romances that describe the history of salvation as a project of God's love for us, culminating in the mother, Mary, who gazes in wonder at the world turned upside down as God gives self to us in love. Although John's experience in Toledo was one of abandonment, cruelty, and total lack of love, he nevertheless wrote the first 31 verses of the love song, the *Spiritual Canticle* that describes the eager search of a bride for her lover. In a dark night, John was fired by love's urgent longings. Although John was only in Toledo for nine months—nine long and painful months, nevertheless, it is the place that captures the agony and the ecstasy of John of the Cross.

Granada: Granada was the last symbol of the 800 year long Muslim power in the Iberian Peninsula. Muhammad XII surrendered to the Catholic Monarchs in 1492 with a treaty that explicitly allowed the Muslim inhabitants to retain their faith and customs. By 1499, Cardinal Cisneros, dissatisfied with the slow efforts at conversions, started a policy of forced baptisms that led to a revolt. By 1501 the crown had rejected the terms of the treaty, and Muslims had to convert or leave the country. Dominating the city was the Alhambra, the residence of the former Muslim rulers of Granada that passed to the Catholic Monarchs on their conquest of all the surrounding areas.

After the conquest, Granada flourished. When the Catholic Monarchs chose it as their base, so too did many Christian families, endowing Granada with wonderful monuments. Granada was one of the largest cities of Spain, but its population began to decline as many Muslims emigrated, and the Moriscos dispersed following the rebellion of 1568-70. On a hill facing the Alhambra lies the El Abaicin, the region of Granada inhabited by the Muslims. As they abandoned their homes, the El Abaicin became more and more a place of green areas.

John lived in Granada for six years (1582-88) as superior of Los Martires, located on the slopes of the Alhambra. A dozen years before his arrival the Moriscos had been driven out following a rebellion. The year he arrived was a year of famine and sterility throughout all Andalusia. When he arrived he was forty years old. The monastery was called Los Martires because tradition commemorates there the martyrdom of 12 Christians by the Moors. Here John enlarged the monastery and constructed an aqueduct with twelve arches to bring water from the Alhambra. In John's time Los Martires was a barren place—the sultans had used it as a convict prison, but in time it became beautiful, secluded, and peaceful.

John lived a very full life in Granada as superior, involved in administration, business, spiritual direction, design and construction work, community building, and endless travel. Granada was the centre of his activities as he traveled extensively—about 8,595 miles, to places such as Almodóvar, Lisbon, Pastrana, Madrid, Bujalance, Valladolid, and Murcia. But he also had time for the spiritual direction of the nuns in Granada and for community life, study, reflection, and writing. During the busiest period with multiple responsibilities, John wrote some of his most wonderful works. As John's prison experience gave rise to his poetry, Granada became the place where he finished the *Ascent of Mount Carmel*, wrote the commentary on the *Dark Night of the Soul* (1582-84), added eight stanzas and wrote his commentary on the *Spiritual Canticle* (1584), and composed both the poem and the commentary on the *Living Flame of Love* (1585).

Reflection points

- *John's search for God contrasts with Philip II's. There are always people who justify whatever they do by claiming it is God's will, but believers know better.*
- *John lived through oppression. People of true values of faith, must maintain their commitment in spite of oppression that can even come from the religious elite, as it did in John's day.*
- *John is above all a person of single-minded commitment to his goals. This world of ours is not a very agreeable place to*

live in. We must stand out against its values, if not publicly, then at least in our own hearts.

The Times in Which John Lived

Spain and Philip II. Philip, who was born in

Valladolid in May 1527, was to become the most powerful monarch in Europe and ruled Spain during most of John's life. He succeeded to the throne of Spain in 1556, when his father, the Holy Roman emperor, Charles V, abdicated. Philip tried always to ingratiate himself to his various subjects, but at the same time he was ruthless and ambitious. His conflicts with the Netherlands and England assumed the character of a religious conflict between Protestantism and Catholicism, and he had further battles with Protestants, Anglicans, Hugenots, and Turks. Philip always presented himself as the champion of the Church, constantly persuading himself that whatever he was doing he was doing for God's glory. Thus, with the Pope's approval he launched the Spanish Armada against Elizabeth's England, a quasi crusade that ended in defeat and the loss of about 15,000 men in 1588.

Philip gave himself wholeheartedly to the reform of the Church in Spain, seeking a more austere reform of religious life even than that recommended by the Council of Trent (1545-63). Philip's approach was not only due to religious enthusiasm but also to the ongoing conflict between papal and royal powers. The fact that Philip sometimes found himself in direct conflict with the pope as ruler of the central section of Italy added to this ongoing separation of powers. Add to this the Carmelite General Congregation's desire for reform and the result is the unbearable mix of representatives of the pope, king, congregation, nuncio, and even the inquisitor. People like John were in the middle of all these jurisdictional conflicts.

Reformation and the Council of Trent.

Martin Luther, a young German Augustinian friar, posted his ninety-five theses on the door of the castle church of Wittenberg on October 31 1517. Initially, his challenge was against the selling of indulgences, but eventually it became a rejection of the medieval view of Church, sacraments, and more. Three years later, in Wittenberg, he rejected the papal challenge, and insisted "Here I stand, I can do no other." On January 3, 1521, he was excommunicated. He died on February 18 1546, the leader of the German reformation that led to the break between Protestantism and Catholicism. There were many abuses within the Roman Church and a clear need for a reformation of head and members. Luther had hoped for an ecumenical council of reform, but the papacy feared any challenge or diminution of its authority. Eventually, Paul III (1534-49), under pressure from Charles V, called the council of Trent in 1545 to deal with the challenges of Protestantism. It was held in Trent, at that time in German territory, even though most participants were Italian, because Paul III wanted to give the impression of an international gathering. Some members, especially German, French, and Spanish, wanted to emphasize reform, but others, especially Roman and Italian, preferred an emphasis on doctrine, feeling that reform efforts would give justification to the Protestant calls for reform in the Church. The council would last until 1563 and have several phases under several popes: Paul III, Julius III (1550-55), Paul IV (1555-59), and Pius IV (1559-64). By the time the council finished its work and published its decrees, the split with Protestantism was irrevocable.

The council's teaching would be of particular interest throughout the lives of Teresa and John. Many of the changes to Teresa's writings, especially her autobiography, were demanded by censors because of Trent's teachings. Moreover, besides the council's teachings, the challenges of the council that secular rulers maintain orthodoxy within their realms would give rise to all kinds of inquisitorial reactions. Teresa and John lived through all these changes in the Church. John went to Salamanca to study theology in 1564 the year after the council of Trent closed.

At a deeper level, the reform of Trent would have a parallel in the spiritual reform of Carmel. The final phase of spiritual renewal leading to Teresa's great conversion of 1554 parallels the preparations and build up to the council of Trent. The culminating points of Trent have correspondence with a new direction in Carmelite reform. John is professed the year the council ends. The ecclesiastical reforms following Trent find parallels in the reforms initiated by Teresa and John; as the leaders of Trent become reformers, so too do Teresa and John.

Perhaps the council's main document was that on justification, which insists that a person is totally transformed by God's justification and not merely externally considered justified as Luther had stated. In the former, grace removes sin, but the latter is a radical denial of the interior supernatural order. Teresa's and John's vivid experiences of God's transforming actions within them become embodiments of Trent's teaching and at the same time real living challenges to Luther's mere external imputation of justice.

The Spanish Inquisition and Orthodoxy.

The Spanish inquisition was originally the work of the Catholic Monarchs (1479), and was charged with seeking out heretics and finding Jews and Muslims who covertly continued to practice their faiths. The first grand inquisitor in Spain was Tomas de Torquemada (1420-98), a fanatic who put to death more than 2,000 people. Eventually, the control over the inquisition passed to Philip II. The intolerance of the inquisition was directed also to Catholics, including the archbishop of Toledo, Bartolomé Carranza, the famous scholar, Luis de León, the great saint and reformer, John of Avila, and Ignatius of Loyola. These famous individuals and lots of ordinary people were persecuted by a few who maintained a rigorous interpretation of what they considered orthodoxy.

In its pursuit of its own view of orthodoxy, the Spanish inquisition carefully watched Christians everywhere; bishops, theologians, scholars, writers, and preachers. They also spied on many people seeking spiritual renewal. Both Teresa and John were reported to the inquisition. One group in particular that the inquisition thought merited oversight was the alumbrados. The term means "illuminated," and followers accepted a more passive interior approach to spiritual renewal and less emphasis on devotion and formal organized religion. It was not a highly organized movement and many people who were unconnected with the movement were accused of sympathy with its views: as John of Avila and Ignatius of Loyola. It was considered a form of quietism, and so Teresa's references to the prayer of quiet readily caused her problems too. Likewise, John's emphasis on passivity caused concern, especially at the time of the publication of his works. In fact, the first edition in 1618 excluded the *Spiritual Canticle* because of it similarity to the *Song of Songs* which the inquisition feared had illuminist tendencies. Moreover, Baeza, where John was rector of the university house of studies, was considered a center for the alumbrados. The alumbrados emphasized recollection, letting go, passivity, and a lack of ecclesiastical control. The inquisition persecuted the alumbrados and then anyone who practiced recollection and mental prayer.

The inquisition's most damaging work was the atmosphere of fear cultivated for everyone, even good dedicated Christians. The inquisition tried to control everyone's belief and religious expression, at times thwarting God's grace and stunting growth. The fact that so many great sixteenth century Spanish saints not only survived the Inquisition but continued to pursue the call of grace is something we can celebrate in faith as the work of the Holy Spirit. Inquisitions continue to this day in every culture.

Carmelite Reform. The fifteenth and sixteenth centuries were times of religious reform in Spain. Several religious communities undertook a return to the more primitive observance of their rules. Mother Teresa began her reform around 1562 when she founded the first house for her community in Avila. In the case of the Carmelites, first nuns and then friars, reform meant going back to the primitive observance and laying aside all the dispensations granted by popes from Eugene IV (1432) onward, and partly as a result of problems caused by decline, the Hundred Years War, schism, abuses in the mendicant orders, and the Black Death. The mitigations were considered a softening of the original vocation, and reform demanded they be laid aside. When Teresa invited John and his first companion, Antonio de Heredia, to join the reform, it essentially meant a return to simplicity, authenticity of Religious Life, austerity, poverty, and contemplation. The fact that this was a homegrown reform that became a new religious order with exclusively Spanish superiors was not lost on Philip II who liked to see his own Spanish Church flourish without interventions from Rome.

Teresa started the reform of the friars with two outstanding individuals, competent, educated, and committed to contemplation—both had indicated their desires to join the Carthusians. Teresa had suffered for many years in her own mediocre religious life and need of conversion and spiritual renewal, and from incompetent spiritual directors. She insisted that both her nuns and friars be knowledgeable of religious issues. Leaders of the reform gave a good theological foundation to the spiritual renewal of their communities, and both Teresa and John wrote extensively, primarily for the formation of the nuns and friars. Teresa was not a trained theologian, but her works were reviewed by outstanding scholars. She also simplified the Divine Office and insisted that it be formative for the nuns, especially in their knowledge of Scripture, and so should be read in the vernacular. John was a trained philosopher and theologian. He knew spiritual theology and Scripture very well. So, the renewal was part of the enthusiasm of the times, but well grounded theologically, biblically, and spiritually. Above all, for John, reform was a daily necessity, as it is in the life of reflective people. Whether you wear sandals and socks (Calced) or not (Discalced) is a not an issue. What is relevant is whether your heart is totally given to God in love.

Reflection points

- *Some people are always afraid of genuine reform. It is frightening that some people fear conversion and religious renewal unless they can control it. John was able to maintain respect while responding uncompromisingly to the call of grace.*
- *Like John, we must all seek to live our values and faith in spite of the trivial controlling influences of the inquisitions of the day. There are always people, generally uninformed, uneducated, and spiritually immature, who want to tell everyone else how to live, what to believe, and how to think. We still have lots of forms of inquisitions especially in so-called free societies where people are still told what is acceptable to believe and say and what is a correct interpretation of current events*
- *John insisted that renewal needs to be grounded in theology, spirituality, and biblical foundations, not the trivial religious issue of the month. Dedicated Christians find that renewal needs solid foundations in the authentic sources of faith.*

John's Own Experiences in Ministry.

John's concern for those in need.

From his earliest years, John always manifested compassionate concern for those in need. He always shared with the poor, even giving them what he himself needed. His hospital service was a well-known aspect of his commitment that he maintained throughout his life, cherishing opportunities to serve the sick. When his brother friars were sick he would go in search of good, nourishing food for them, even delicacies, to raise their bodies and spirits. Likewise, John was generous in providing help and nourishment to those who were poor, needy, and sick spiritually. Thus, from the earliest weeks in Duruelo, John went out to minister with the spiritual and sacramental means of confession and to feed with religious instruction those in the region who needed spiritual strengthening. John knew how to be without things and could recommend it to others. "I didn't know you, my Lord, because I still desired to know and relish things" (S. 33).

John also drew qualities out of people who had not shown them previously. Thus, from the times in Medina del Campo up to the years in Baeza, Granada, and Segovia, John helped people understand how their generosity to the less fortunate would enrich their own lives, and so, they also willingly provided financial support to the needy. At times, John gave instruction to those who needed it by not responding to their requests, or by not accepting their gifts, thereby clarifying priorities of simplicity and sufficiency over abundance.

John was a person of single-minded dedication to the ministry of leading others to a deeper relationship with God. In all he did, this was his only goal. He encouraged and supported those with whom he traveled. He was always first to respond to needs in the community. He was careful to correct exaggerations that some imposed on themselves in their spiritual journey. What is clear is that more than anything else he loved people and had a natural gift, enriched by grace, of treating everyone with a benevolence that anticipated their basic yearning for goodness. This made him very concerned about people, perennially compassionate, always seeking their greater good.

These fundamental attitudes and wide-ranging influence come out on every page of his writings. He not only writes to address people's specific needs, but his writing is the fruit of his loving interaction with many people. When he gives examples he seems without a doubt to have someone specific in mind. When you read John, you always think he is talking to someone in particular. John's ministry seldom consists in lectures and talks to groups, rather his is one on one, hours at a time if necessary. He gets to know his directees. Clearly, John's letters continue his supportive presence to others, and his *Sayings of Light and Love*, left in each person's place in the dining room, gave firm indication of his thoughtfulness and love and were again a form of ongoing direction.

John's major works including the *Dark Night* are filled with wisdom that came from working with people. Reflection on his own experience and theirs too led him to an integrated approach to spiritual healing. Moreover no spiritual writer has so clearly applied the seven deadly sins to the spiritual realm as has John of the Cross. Even though he speaks of darkness, nakedness, deprivation, and self-conquest, he appears as a master of human nature, knowing its weaknesses and its strengths.

John's ministry to friars and nuns of the reform. We have seen John's tireless efforts on behalf of the reform of both friars and nuns. From Duruelo to Pastrana and Mancera de Abajo, and later El Calvario, Los Martires, and Segovia, John was always involved in formation work, as novice master or superior. Likewise, John spent fruitful years as chaplain of the monastery of the Incarnation in Avila, and throughout the rest of his life became the most important spiritual guide of the reformed nuns, whether in Beas, in Granada, throughout Andalusia during his travels, and in Segovia. John used his own experiences and reflections to help both friars and nuns, sharing his poetry with them as he did in Toledo immediately following his escape. His major works are also written primarily at their request. Thus, at the beginning of the *Ascent of Mount Carmel* he says: "My main intention is not to address everyone, but only some of the persons of our holy order of the primitive observance of Mount Carmel, both friars and nuns, whom God favors by putting them on the path leading to this mount, since they are the ones who asked me to write this work" (A. Prologue.9).

At times, John was asked to resolve some particularly difficult issues. He was sent to Pastrana to intervene regarding excessive practices of penance. In Avila, he called a nun to conversion and paid the price in a beating from a man who sought her attention and affection. John also became known as a dedicated exorcist, most notable in the case of the Augustinian nun, Maria de Olivares, but in others too. In Segovia, Fr. Doria asked John to evaluate the authenticity of the spirit and prayer of an unnamed nun, and he censured her on account of five defects he found in her account.

As mentioned above, the *Sayings of Light and Love* prolong John's ministry to his directees. From the time he was chaplain at the Incarnation, John established the practice of distributing to his directees and penitents small cards with a spiritual maxim to focus their commitment. Later, when provincial vicar in Andalusia, and unable to give as much time as he wanted to the nuns of the Teresian reform, he would leave each of them some short written advice. These sayings are an excellent example of how John applied his teachings to the specific needs of individuals and how he could condense his vision in a single statement.

John wrote the *Precautions* for the nuns in Beas, during the time when he was the confessor (1578-79). They contain a lot of practical wisdom and while they have application beyond religious life, they are a fine summary of his teachings in a short form for the nuns in Beas, and they can be a preparation for the passive purification of spirit. Although directed to the nuns these *Precautions*—in the copy we have—are addressed in the masculine, thereby possibly indicating that they are a copy made for the friars. This would not be surprising, since the *Sayings of Light and Love* were also copied and redistributed.

John also wrote many letters to nuns and friars of which we have 33 (or 32). This correspondence gives us insight into concrete applications of his teachings to people he knew and loved. Some themes are frequent: the night, the spirit of poverty, the love of God, silence, and solitude.

John's ministry to laity of his day.

John's ministry was not just directed to members of the reform. Lay people played a major role in his life, as friends, spiritual directees, advisors, and partners in ministry. In the earliest days of the reform John met Blas de Medina, a merchant, Don Rafael Mejia Velasquez, a prominent Avilan, and Francisco de Salcedo. The married woman, Doña Ana del Mercado y Peñalosa likewise played a crucial role in John's life, and in the spread of the Carmelite reform in Andalusia. A wealthy widow, she assisted John and Ann of Jesus in establishing a monastery of Discalced Carmelite nuns in Granada. She became one of John's closest friends and the directee for whom he wrote and to whom he dedicated the *Living Flame of Love*, his most sublime work. She later returned to her original palace in Segovia, becoming the principal benefactress of the Discalced Carmelite monastery in that city. When John was eventually transferred to Segovia himself, she left her palace to live in some small buildings directly across the road from the monastery, so that she could be closer to her director. In fact, as a reward for her generosity, she obtained permission to be buried there in the Carmelite chapel next to her husband, so that no matter where John of the Cross would die he too would be buried in the same place. In addition to the *Living Flame*, John wrote two letters to Doña Ana (28 and 31). These writings indicate John's profound appreciation for this "noble and devout lady." These letters show John's concern for her friendship and health, while the *Living Flame*, the description of the later stages in the spiritual life, shows how deeply he knew and appreciated her spiritual and mystical maturity.

In fact, as John moved to various cities he always attracted the friendship and spiritual commitment of laity. In Baeza there were Teresa de Ibros (a farm laborer's wife and mystic), Maria de Paz, Maria Vilches, Juana de Arjona, Juana de la Paz, Bernadina de Robles, Juan de Vera (a sculptor and painter). In Segovia there were Doña Ana del Mercado y Penalosa, her niece Ines (mentioned in letter 31) and her maid Leonor de Vitoria. In Granada lived Juana de Padraza, to whom John wrote two of his surviving letters (11 and 19). In the first he expresses genuine friendship and his delight in receiving letters from her, and also speaks of love of God and obedience to the divine will in ways that presume Juana's spiritual maturity. In Ubeda John's friends, directees, and benefactors included Doña Maria de Molina and her two daughters, Catalina and Inez, Doctor Villarreal, Don Bartolomé Ortega Cabrio, Cristobal de la Higuera, Juan de Cuellar, and many others. John also attracted many young people to his spiritual guidance, and while some of them may have later become priests or religious, it was as laity that the initial commitment was made; Juan de San Pablo, Luis de San Angelo, José de la Madre de Dios, Sabastián de San Hilario. Clearly in his own day John was close to lay people, who valued his friendship and guidance.

Given the social and religious environment of his day and his own interests in the reform, it is to be expected that John would have directed his attention primarily to the friars and nuns. However, it is equally clear that John found many laity attracted to his teaching and ready to receive his guidance. Laity could readily identify with John, even though he was wholeheartedly committed to the austerities of the reform. They could identify with his view of family life, his spirituality of work, his ability to integrate community recreation into his life, his capacity for friendship, his ability to survive amidst both the strengths and weaknesses of the Church's life, his purity of intention and rootedness in the uncluttered core of Christian spiritual life. John struck a cord and continues to do so in the lives of laity. Any interpretation of his teachings must keep in mind that he readily applied them to laity with a frequency beyond what could be considered exceptional; rather he presumed his teachings had a natural application to laity as well as religious.

Reflection points

- *John's extraordinary love and concern for people in their material and spiritual needs reminds all of us of the overriding imperative that as Christians we must be known for our love and service.*
- *Each of us has a particular calling, a destiny in this world that no one else can fulfill if not us. For John it consisted primarily in his ministry to the reform. Each of us must discover what our destiny is.*
- *Sometimes what we might think is a restricted ministry opens up to the service of others in an extraordinary way we could never have anticipated. For John, laity in his generation and in every generation since, and especially in our own, feel called by John's vision and challenge. In a smaller way our ministry can be like his.*

The Writings of John of The Cross

John's ministry of the written word.

We have seen that John, who was above all a mystic, shared his knowledge of the spiritual journey to God through his spiritual direction. He directed people from all walks of life, religious men and women, clergy, and laity; young people, the poor, wealthy merchants, benefactors, and the nobility of the day. John did not seem to have any inclination to write. His books are written in response to frequent requests. After his imprisonment in Toledo, John's ministry took on a new dimension when he started to direct others through his major writings—clearly he had already done this through the maxims he left for his directees. Both in the Toledo prison and after, John spontaneously wrote poetry for his own support and consolation. Thus, during the brutal experience in prison John wrote the first 31 stanzas of the *Spiritual Canticle*, the "Romances," and two very beautiful poems. His prose work came later. He apparently did not write much in his last years. So John's oral teaching and spiritual direction preceded, accompanied, and followed his written magisterium. All his writings show a spiritual maturity, the result of personal experiences and years of directing others, as we saw in the above section.

There are about a thousand pages of John's work in most modern editions, which is not much when compared to other Doctors of the Church. No originals of his writings remain, although we have an autograph copy of the *Sayings*. His writings can be classified into three groups: First, his four major works are poetry and prose together—he explains the poems in a commentary. A second group of writings are exclusively poetry—about three hundred stanzas altogether; these include ten "Romances," or ballards, five poetical glosses, and two other poems. And finally we have several shorter prose works, including the *Sayings of Light and Love*,

Precautions, Counsels to a Religious, Censure and Opinion, and thirty three letters. There were other writings that people claimed to have seen, but they have not come down to us

As mentioned already, John spontaneously wrote poetry to express his inner mystical experiences. He could then return to the poems to rekindle the original experience or to gain perspective in moments of anguish. At times he wrote because someone asked him to explain his poetry. Thus, he explained the stanzas of the *Spiritual Canticle* because Mother Ann of Jesus, prioress of the discalced Carmelites in Granada, asked him to. Likewise the commentary on the *Living Flame of Love* was written in response to a request from Doña Ana of Peñalosa. Often his letters include answers to specific requests from directees. Sometimes John wrote because he wanted to help resolve real needs he saw, as is the case with the *Ascent of Mount Carmel.* John saw his writing as a genuine expression of his own ministry. As we look back over centuries and appreciate his influence in the lives of so many, we can agree.

John's poetry. In writing poetry John seems to have been influenced by forms current in his day and by at least three important Spanish poets: Garcilasco, Boscán, and Sebastián de Cordoba. He used the meters of the day, followed the *villancico* in which the last line of the introductory verse is repeated throughout—as in "For I know well the spring," which ends each stanza with "although it is night," and also the practice found in religious communities of taking a secular poem and transposing it to a religious level (a lo divino)—as he does in "A lone young shepherd." John also followed others in his emphasis on pastoral themes and on the storyline of the "Canticle of Canticles."

The "Romances" are an important part of John's theological synthesis and focus on God's self-gift to us in salvation history, instead of on our return journey to God, such as we find in the four major works of John. Focusing on God's plan for the world, they complement the seeker's return journey to God. The nine interlinked "Romances" present poetical reflections on the Trinity and the Incarnation. Important for their doctrinal synthesis, their simple and beautifully expressed doctrines are rich in their biblical, Trinitarian, Christological, and ecclesiological understanding and vision.

"I went out seeking love" is a gloss that substitutes the image of hunting for prey instead of longing for love. It is a secular poem to which John gives a religious interpretation of hope. "Without support yet with support" is a secular poem to which John gives a religious interpretation; the disciple, dissatisfied with every creature, longs for the love of God. The three stanzas successively focus on faith, hope, and charity. "Not for all beauty" is yet another secular poem that takes on an extraordinary meaning for John, who identifies beauty with the essence of God. Once a disciple has tasted the beauty of God, nothing else will ever bring satisfaction.

In addition to the "Romances," the glosses, and the poems on which he bases his major works, John wrote two further poems of exceptional beauty. "For I know well the spring," describes how a disciple rejoices in knowing God through faith. Written during John's time in prison in Toledo, this poem was probably written on the octave of the feast of Corpus Christi. Having been deprived of the Eucharist for six months and living in darkness, John gives the poem an extraordinary doctrinal development from the inner life of the Trinity to the gift of the Eucharist. "A lone young shepherd" is a beautiful love poem that John uses to express the love between Christ and the disciple. By changing only the last verse, John gives new meaning to the whole poem which now culminates in the loving surrender of Christ on the cross.

John's shorter works of prose. Among John's shorter prose compositions we find the *Sayings of Light and Love,* a collection of spiritual maxims that John used to give to his directees who then often copied them and passed them on to others. So, we now have several collections of these sayings. The structure of the sayings is very simple but not monotonous, and many are extraordinary in successfully condensing John's spiritual vision in a single statement. Some are quite poetical (16), some are maxims for life (60), advice in confronting dangers (66), prayer (50), or confession (39). The major themes of the sayings are the necessity of spiritual direction, denial of one's appetites, the importance of being guided by reason rather than by feeling or taste, the nature of authentic love, and intimacy with God. One saying that is sometimes included with the others but not always is the "Prayer of a Soul Taken with Love." This saying, which some writers consider autobiographical, develops in a continuing crescendo from the misery of sin, to humble abandonment, to confidence in Jesus, and finally to the enthusiastic possession of everything in the Lord.

The "Precautions" are a group of nine norms to keep in mind in order to avoid the typical dangers in spiritual life—the classical enemies, world, devil, and flesh. Every precaution has a similar structure: a warning, advantages from observing the warning, harm from its omission. Against threats from the world John advises detachment; against threats from the devil John recommends obedience to one's director; and against threats from weaknesses of the flesh John urges that we seek that which is least desirable.

In "Counsels to a Religious on How to Reach Perfection" John offers four counsels: resignation, mortification, practice of virtue, and solitude. Finally, we have about 33 of John's letters which give us insight into concrete applications of his teachings to individuals. Included with the letters is sometimes found the "Censure and Opinion" that was mentioned above.

John's four major works are the *Ascent of Mount Carmel*, the *Dark Night of the Soul*, the *Spiritual Canticle*, and the *Living Flame of Love*. All four deal with aspects of the whole journey to God. The first two use the image of the night and describe especially the journey of faith, whereas the

Spiritual Canticle and the *Living Flame* use matrimonial or nuptial imagery and stress the journey of love.

Reflection points

- *John had the ability to extend his ministry to others in a variety of creative ways—poetry, maxims, detailed commentaries. He was a model of doing the greatest good possible with whatever means he had.*

- *John, "the greatest poet of the Spanish language," draws us into the joy and excitement of the journey to God. We should read his poems frequently as the best summary of his teachings.*

- *John's major works present us with the journey of faith and the journey of love. These are not a choice, both are necessary. The journey culminates in love.*

John – A Prophet of God

We often mistakenly think a prophet speaks about the future, but this function is minor and accidental to the prophet's main task. The word "prophet" comes from Greek and means to speak on behalf of God. A prophet challenges people to live in the present according to the values of God, and surely there are few people to whom this applies more than John of the Cross. The influences on his life are at times unusual, but he pursues his goal of union with God in love no matter the circumstances. At times his is a voice in the wilderness proclaiming the wonders of God and calling us all to faithfully pursue transformative union even through the nights of life.

John lived with many people who had a wrong set of values. Whether they were political leaders who saw greatness in expansionism, wars, power, and wealth, or religious leaders forcing conversions, controlling other people's belief, and imposing their own views on others. Likewise the social caste system stressed wealth, status, bloodlines as important aspects of life. John lived with people who were attached to the structures that gave them power and prestige. John understood how useless it was to force belief systems on people who did not want them. All around him he saw people creating God in their own image and likeness, unwilling to let go and let God be a transforming presence in their lives. A prophet condemns such warped views of humanity and challenges us to follow God, for faith needs to be a loving self-gift

John was poor in spirit, or even more, poor with spirit. He loved being poor and appreciated how this could lead to greatness. He lived peacefully in spite of religious corruption all around him. In fact, he always lived with love for the Church with its awkwardness and with its graciousness. He knew that even bad situations have potentiality for good, and he sought such goodness amidst the horrors inflicted on him. It is amazing how John kept focused on his goals of union with God no matter the circumstances around him. But, he was practical too, and knew when enough is enough; so he knew when it was time to escape from the prison that the religiously arrogant had created for him.

As a prophet of God, John above all told us how to see God's love everywhere, in nature, in people, and even in oppressors. John appreciated his own enduring purpose in life, his own destiny. He yearned for transformation in loving union with God. John pursued spiritual growth but never selfishly, rather always with a sensitivity and compassion towards everyone he met. He was not a lonely mystic in selfish pursuit of perfection. He was a man for others; enjoying others' company, facilitating their growth, and seeking whatever was best for them. More than anything, this prophet lived his life aware of a realm of life beyond this one that gave meaning to this one. No matter the situations of his day and the nights he had to live, John speaks of God and reminds us the nights might be dark, but they can be guiding, transforming, and beautiful.

CHAPTER THREE
AIDS TO READING THE
DARK NIGHT

We have come to know John a little more in the dark nights of his own life, hard experiences that formed and transformed him. We concluded that John is an inspiration for us in our journeys through the nights. We have also considered a group of influences that made John who he was, and we delighted in recognizing him as a prophet who calls us to be faithful to God's ways in our own lives. We now consider some aids to reading our chosen book, the *Dark Night*. We need to locate the doctrine within John's overall system. Since there are clear indications that John saw the *Dark Night* as Book IV of the *Ascent*, we want to constantly see the links between these two works. John uses mystical language to express the ineffable mysteries of God, and we must be aware of how he uses it and why. Moreover, there are a set of concepts that are important to John, and we need to understand them as he intended and not in any other way. Finally, we will review some practical suggestions for reading John. Above all if we want to really benefit from our reading of the *Dark Night* we should cultivate a sense of enthusiasm for John, his guidance, and his teachings.

Appreciate John's System of Spiritual Growth

When John of the Cross writes any of his works his system of spiritual development is already complete, at least in his own mind. He may write other works later, but these are explanations for others not for him. Everyone lives based on convictions that form a systematic way of approaching life—whether they realize it or not, whether they can articulate them or not. John has a very clear understanding of the systematic development of the spiritual life and how each part relates to others in a progressive development. Part of John's genius is his ability to see the whole picture. Thus, he can refer to a dark night, a guiding night, and a night more lovely than the dawn. He can see suffering as an integral part of total transformation. He may start by saying "I went out unseen," "I went out calling you," and "tear through the veil,"—all first steps in the journey whose challenges, blessings, and end he already knows. So, when John writes to his directees he locates his advice within the context of the systematic development of the spiritual life (see L. 3 and 13, S. 19, 23, 25).

There are other signs that John sees a specific purpose for each step in the whole development process. He speaks of the benefits of the nights when he has already moved on to something better, and thus no longer feels the burden but the resulting joy. "One dark night, . . . ah, the sheer grace!" "This glad night and purgation causes many benefits, even though to the soul it seemingly deprives it of them" (N.1. 12.1). This ability to see the overall picture also gives rise to the sometimes contrasting reactions of John and his directees, real or literary. Beginners rejoice in their initial consolations, but John is saddened by their lowly state. Those in the passive night suffer, while John, knowing what is really happening, can rejoice. A further sign of the presence of a system in John's works is his continual use of parenthetical remarks to clarify what is happening. Some asides refer to what lies ahead (A.2. 5.1), others to stages already passed (F. 1.18; C. Theme.1).

While his major works refer to our return journey to God, John is also very clear about what precedes our journey to God, namely, God's journey to us, brilliantly described in the "Romances." Our journey to God is modeled on God's journey to us. John is always aware of God's strategy of love, both in coming to us and in drawing us to divine life. John is a wonderful guide; he knows the major steps in our journey even though they may not be entirely predictable, nor identical for all. But a prudent guide like John knows the key moments in our journey to God; he already knows possible pitfalls, challenges, moments of rest, and the ecstasy of the end.

Some disciples of John see his system as a modification of Pseudo-Denis the Areopagite's division of the spiritual journey into three stages: beginners, proficient, and perfect, corresponding to the purgative, illuminative, and unitive phases of spiritual growth. John accepts these stages, but stresses the transitions from one to the other in the night of sense and the night of spirit.

Others feel John's system starts with souls who have already made a decisive commitment to God and hence he excludes the preliminaries of spiritual preparation and focuses on the means to the end of union with God. The means are the nights seen in three steps: 1. the active night of sense, 2. the active night of spirit and the passive night of sense taken together as two aspects of the same experience, and 3. the passive night of spirit.[4]

A simple way of understanding John's thought which is the secret of his own life and his system is to view life as a dynamic development in three fundamental phases: the relentless pursuit of God, the willingness to endure the nights, and the discovery of union with God which is also the total renewal of self. In this view, the spiritual journey implies emptying ourselves of all that is not God, so that we can be filled with what is truly of God. For John the focus is not on the negative aspects of the means but on the enthusiasm for the end in transformative love. In fact, the whole system is nothing except decisions of choice-oriented love, always choosing what is the most loving thing to do.

John presented his overview of the spiritual life in a diagram of the ascent of Mount Carmel. John offered this diagram as a visual synthesis of his views (see A.1. 13.10), and he made several copies for disciples. The mountain has three valleys that seem to lead to the top. Two wide valleys on each side—the valley of earthly goods and the valley of heavenly goods—are ways people think will lead them to God but they do not—in some diagrams the two valleys are closed at the end. The center valley is the narrow and difficult road of self-emptying, but this is the shortcut, the assured way to the top of the mountain. This center path is not a smooth ascent, but has many ups and downs along the way. "The soul, if it desires to pay close attention, will clearly recognize how on this road it suffers many ups and downs, and how immediately after prosperity some tempest and trial follows, so much so that seemingly the calm was given to forewarn and strengthen it against the future penury" (N.2. 18.3).

See the Links Between the Ascent and the Dark Night

Although each has a distinct title, the *Ascent* and the *Dark Night* together form one work, which must be understood as a unity in life and doctrine. The two works complement each other; the *Ascent* deals with the active nights and the *Dark Night* with the passive nights. While the *Ascent* utilizes the diagram of Mount Carmel as a didactic aid, both works comment on the poem "One Dark Night." The two works form a diptych, two parts of the one unique active-passive journey to God.

In the *Ascent* (A.1. 1.3) John explains the division of his treatise: the active night of sense in Book I, the active night of spirit in Books II and III, and "In the fourth section we will discuss the night insofar as it is passive." This fourth part of the *Ascent* is actually the book of the *Dark Night*. The first night of the sensory part, the active night of sense (*Ascent*), happens to beginners when they choose love and virtue over the pleasure pain principle of gratification and are gradually drawn into contemplation. The second night, of the spiritual part (*Dark Night*), "takes place in those who are already proficients" (A.1. 1.3).[5] Again in *Ascent* (A.3. 2.14) John indicates that the journey to God is only completed in the passive night of spirit of which he says he will speak later— that becomes books I and II of the *Dark Night*. In *Ascent* (A.2. 18.4) John says he is going to deal with the seven deadly sins, but he does so only in the *Dark Night* (N.2-7; see also A.2. 6.8). In the *Dark Night* (N.2. 22.2) John refers to what he said in the prologue, but he is referring to the prologue of the *Ascent* (A. Prologue.3). So, John often speaks in the *Ascent* as if his intention was to make the *Dark Night* a fourth book. In fact, in *Living Flame* (F. 1.25) he says "In the Dark Night of the Ascent of Mount Carmel" he dealt with the intensity of the passive purgation. In general, we can say that the *Dark Night* continues the *Ascent*, but we need to also acknowledge they are generally published separately.

Although both commentaries claim to explain the eight stanzas of the poem (see N. Prologue), *Ascent* does not go beyond the last line of stanza 2, and *Dark Night* stops suddenly one line further on, "on that glad night." So, the six remaining stanzas that describe the illuminative stage and the stage of union receive no commentary. It is hardly appropriate to say John left his work incomplete. It is not like John to go on and write the *Spiritual Canticle* and the *Living Flame*, not even at the insistence of two such important people as Ann of Jesus and Doña Ana of Peñalosa, without finishing his previous work. Moreover, although the *Dark*

Night has an excitement about it that the *Ascent* does not, giving the impression this is what John really wants to talk about, it seems unlikely John would leave aside an incomplete *Ascent* to get to the subject matter of the *Dark Night*.[6] In general it seems the answer is simply John felt he had adequately dealt with the content of what would have been central to the last stanzas of the poem, and so he felt it appropriate to end. He had achieved what he set out to do (see N.2. 22.1-2).

It is also important to note that the poem "One Dark Night" and the sketch of the mountain both come from the period John spent in El Calvario, Beas, and Baeza (1578-81). John began the commentary on the *Ascent* in El Calvario (around 1581-85) and he could possibly have begun the commentary on the *Dark Night* while still in Baeza, developing it in Granada (1584-85). In other words both works are in phases of preparation around the same time, thereby allowing John to mature his thought on both together.

Both works are intimately connected and we need to study both to have a complete picture. They each do have a distinct focus: *Ascent* is active and *Dark Night* is passive. But we cannot maintain too rigid a separation since much of the active night of spirit is directly related to the passive night of sense, being two facets of one experience. Then the experience of *Ascent* is foundational for the experience of the *Dark Night*, and generally the active nights begin before the passive nights but then continue through life. Moreover, the purgation of the passive nights also continues the purgation begun in the active nights, uprooting any attachments that may still remain.

As we study the *Dark Night* we need to keep in mind the links between these two great works. They both have similar themes—faith, darkness, night, nakedness, purification, contemplation, love, union with God. Both treat the same overriding theme of a journey through darkness to loving union with God. Acknowledging their similarities we must nevertheless let each work speak to us in its own way. *Ascent* speaks of effort, difficulties, determination, activity, and preparations. *Dark Night* speaks of loneliness, uprooting, abandonment, emptiness, expectations, passivity, and silence. We can appreciate their connections while letting each one speak to us as John wished.

Be Aware of John's Mystical Language

Language is so important to us for communication, development of relationships, and our own growth as human beings. It is particularly important in matters of religion where we transmit vital experiences through the language of faith. Sometimes expressions of faith end up as just words, and we then lose the reality behind the words. So, when we seek to express spiritual realities we often use concepts from the Bible, church doctrine, speculative theology, even ideas from nature or other religions. For the mystic, all these are inadequate; for one cannot fully explain what one has experienced in God's loving gifts. Thus, John comments on the efforts of some who went before him. "The saintly doctors, no matter how much they have said or will say, can never furnish an exhaustive explanation of these figures and comparisons, since the abundant meanings of the Holy Spirit cannot be caught in words. Thus, the explanation of these expressions usually contains less than what they embody in themselves" (C. Prologue.1).

Conceptual and speculative language may help to clarify and articulate our faith, but its vital core—our loving relationship with God—is more truly shared "in mystical theology which is known through love and by which these truths are not only known but at the same time enjoyed" (C. Prologue.3). People who have had a profound spiritual experience generally find it difficult to explain it to others in precise language. Often this is because they do not fully understand it themselves, or their explanation always seems to fall far short of the experience. John himself pointed this out, "everything I say is as far from reality as is a painting from the living object represented" (F. Prologue.1). But he also suggests, "For mystical wisdom, which comes through love. . . need not be understood distinctly in order to cause love and affection in the soul, for it is given according to the mode of faith through which we love God without understanding him" (C. Prologue.2). Because of this difficulty, mystics often use figurative expressions rather than rational explanations. "These persons let something of their experience overflow in figures, comparisons, and similitudes, and from the abundance of their spirit pour out secrets and mysteries rather then rational explanations" (C. Prologue.1).

John's major works begin with figurative titles—ascent, dark night, canticle of love, living flame—titles that already evoke responses in the hearts of believers. John then presents his poems as glimpses into his profound experiences: "unable to express the fullness of his meaning in ordinary words, [he] utters mysteries in strange figures and likenesses" (C. Prologue.1). When disciples ask John to explain these poems he starts with a prologue in which he states that it is not possible to explain adequately the experiences to which the poems refer. "I have felt somewhat reluctant . . . to explain these four stanzas. . . since they deal with matters so interior and spiritual, for which words are usually lacking. . . I find it difficult to say something of their content...." (F. Prologue.1; see also A. Prologue.1 and C. Prologue.2).

Given this drawback of ordinary language, mystics often choose poetry as a natural form to express the mysteries of God. Finding the experience ineffable, indescribable, mystics use the transformative and transcendent language of poetry which is generally synthetic, global, creative, and always open to new meanings at other times. Where poetry is not possible, mystics often use suggestive language. Thus, when a mystic says he or she is willing to die a thousand deaths to repeat their experience of God, they tell us how wonderful was the joy they felt in the experience (see C. 9.2-3). In addition to poetry and hyperbole, mystics use symbols—images that bring together a set of characteristics and evoke a precise response. Examples of such symbols in John would be fire, light, night, nature, and matrimony. When dealing with symbols the reader must first identify with the symbol being used, it must immediately evoke the reality it represents, but at the same time the reader must rise from the immediate symbolic expression to think of transcendent reality.

Our interest lies particularly in John's use of the symbol of the night; it is his main symbol and he uses it 247 times. In the Old Testament night was a sign of the presence of God to the chosen people—in the night God guided the people with a pillar of fire. We have also seen how John's life was filled with experiences of the night. Night takes on the meaning of darkness, mystery, uncertainty, torment, as well as adventure, risk, and the light of dawn. For John, night describes the whole spiritual journey: dark night, glad night, tranquil night, guiding night, serene night, night more lovely than the dawn, and night that has united the Lover with his beloved. It is the context in which the whole of life develops, and after each stage John can always say "although it is night." John has very definite reasons why he uses night as we shall see (A.1. 2.1). It is interesting to see just how successful John's use of the term night has been, since nowadays people from all walks of life use the term "dark night" and everyone has some idea what it means.

Appreciating mystical language in its many expressions requires ascetical commitment. "Spiritual joy directed to God at the sight of all divine or profane things follows from the eye already purged of enjoyment in seeing things" (A.3. 26.5). So, as we read John, we must remember that "these words are spirit and life. These words are perceived by souls who have ears to hear them, those souls, as I say that are cleansed and enamored" (F. 1.5).

Keep In Mind Some Important Concepts

John's view of a person. We have seen that John has a great love for people. However, he always views each one as a person in need of transformation. At times his descriptions seem pessimistic and discouraging regarding a person's future hopes (A.1. 6-10; A.3. 19; N.1. 2; N.2. 2). John does not despise a person, but he understands the depth of sin and sinful tendencies that prevent the growth he would like to see. At the same time the goal he offers each person is more optimistic than that found in lesser spiritualities. In our journey to God John sees the starting point as lower, the journey longer, and the goal much higher—great opportunities for grace, call, and response.

John accepts the traditional division of a person into body and soul, five external senses, three internal spiritual faculties (intellect, memory, and will), and four passions (fear, hope, joy, and sorrow). John is concerned that each faculty, if not purified and rectified, can negatively affect the whole person, and in his vision of the total transformation of a person he believes it is indispensible to redirect to good each faculty individually.

Basically he sees a person as motivated by two forces, sense and spirit: sense refers to the "inferior part," meaning exterior, natural, sensitive. Whereas spirit refers to the "superior part," interior, supernatural, and spiritual. However, and this is important for John, he sees these divisions dynamically and not statically. Sense is not power, money, sex, and selfishness; spirit is not prayer, liturgy, devotions, and religion. For John, sense refers to the whole person when led by forces that move one away from God, and spirit refers to the whole person when all life is directed to God (A.3. 26.3)

People without John's perception have often given the impression that to spend time in prayer, spiritual direction, liturgy, and so on is religiously better than to spend time in work, family life, conjugal growth, societal development. John is not interested in conquering and directing one aspect of life, his goal is the transformation of the whole person, to produce a totally God-directed life. We have seen how many married laity he knew who directed their lives totally to God and how often he found religious people selfishly motivated in the pursuit of religion. After all, John is one of the very few spiritual writers to interpret the seven deadly sins on a spiritual level.

John's insight into a dynamic view of a person is enlightening. Put simply, a person can direct the whole of life to God (money, sex, power, liturgy, prayer, devotions, etc) or can direct the whole of life to self gratification (not only money, sex, power, but also liturgy, prayer, devotions, etc). However, while John's concept is revolutionary, he still uses the old language of sense and spirit. We must be careful not to interpret statically for a part what he intends dynamically for the whole.

Mystical life and contemplation. John understands both concepts in broader terms than other spiritual writers, including Teresa. Generally, the distinction between ascetical and mystical depends on whether one is actively involved as in ascetical effort or passively moved by God as in mystical gift. Teresa's first three mansions in the *Interior Castle* and the advice and guidance in the *Way of Perfection* are part of one's ascetical life of good moral living and meditative, discursive prayer. The mystical phase of life begins with the fourth mansion, where she refers to the prayer of quiet—"quiete" being Latin for "at rest." The ascetical phase is effort-filled, whereas the mystical is passively received.

John has a broader understanding of the notion of mystical life. He wishes to stress the divine influences on the soul, influences that can be hidden and imperceptible. However, at all stages in the spiritual life we are being drawn by God's grace, even though our acceptance and response can imply effort on our part. John speaks at length about prayer (see as an example A.2. 12-15 where he gives the transition signs from meditation to contemplation). He speaks of the prayer of recollection, or acquired recollection but what he describes in the early stages of prayer cannot be identified with the prayer of quiet, and God is not passively moving the individual. For Teresa contemplation is always infused and equal even in the early stages to the prayer of quiet. John's description leads to an understanding of two phases of recollection, acquired and infused. This has been much debated by schools of spirituality, but the early phases of contemplation, while being gift and therefore infused, require real cooperation by an individual. When in active recollection a person is quiet by his or her own initiative, actively attends to being simply present to God, and is aware of his or her own contribution (see F. 3.33). These are the transition signs that refer to proficients moving from meditation to infused recollection and contemplation.

John's approach to this early phase of more interior prayer is more within our reach and makes it attainable by ordinary means of grace. It is active, common, and ordinary, and is a preparation for infused contemplation. John even suggests one should move back and forth between this recollection when attained and regular meditation when that seems appropriate. "We did not mean that those beginning to have this general loving knowledge should never again try to meditate. In the beginning of this state the habit of contemplation is not so perfect that one can at will enter into this act, neither is one so remote from discursive meditation as to be always incapable of it" (A.2. 15.1). So, he calls this early phase of contemplation "this general loving knowledge," and points out it is not always possible "that one can at will enter into this act."

So, for John, both concepts of mystical contemplative life and contemplative prayer cover wider ranges of spiritual life than explanations found in many other writers. As we read John's works we should keep this in mind and not interpret narrowly what John conceives broadly.

Attachment and detachment. These two concepts are found throughout John's writings, as he urges us to be detached from anything that moves us away from God, and continually warns against attachments to objects that diminish our focus within God. John dislikes the thought that our spiritual energy be divided and thereby weakened as we pursue several attachments. "The appetites sap strength needed for perseverance in the practice of virtue. Because the force of the desire is divided, the appetite becomes weaker than if it were completely fixed on one object" (A.1. 10.1; and see all A.1. 10). Perhaps John's frequent use of this idea can be summed up with his advice, "If you purify your soul of attachments and desires, you will understand spiritually. If you deny your appetite for them you will enjoy their truth, understanding what is certain in them" (S. 49, see also 22, 24).

John's goal is not detachment but rather freedom for reception of God in mutual self-giving. "[Y]ou have not only drawn my soul away from all things, but have also made it go out from self. . . and you have raised it up to yourself while it was calling after you, now totally detached so as to be attached to you" (C. 1.20). John is concerned about attachment to objects outside of God whereby the object takes possession of the person as an end in itself (see A.3. 20.3). Thus, he speaks against attachment that leads to "joy in creatures," when what he seeks is "freedom of the heart for God" (A.3. 20.4), space for God to come into.

John lived at a time when temporal, earthly realities were viewed negatively. Rather, people should focus on heavenly values and not be tainted by this world. Hence, the frequently used concept in spiritual writings of "flight from the world" (fuga mundi). This led to an approach to spiritual development that disdained the world, despised ordinary everyday life, and viewed the flight to the monasteries as the best goal in life. People who could not become monks or nuns would even build their homes as close to the monastery wall as possible, join a third order, even seek the privilege of being buried in monastic robes. All indicated the movement of detachment from this world and its values and an exclusive appreciation for values of the otherworld.

John loved friends and family, delighted in the beauty of nature, cherished study, books, poetry, writing, valued the restorative aspects of good food for his sick brothers, and so on. There is no way one can say John despised the goods of this world. Moreover, John does not focus detachment solely on the goods of this world. Rather, he is well aware that spiritual life can be stunted by choices based on the gratification principle of attachment to heavenly goods "and the gratification [is] found in spiritual things" (N.1. 13.1).

A careful reading of John shows he is primarily seeking a unified affective focus on total self-gift to God. He uses the language of attachment and detachment because that was current in his day. The Church is now at a different point than in John's time, having defined the autonomy of earthly realities in the Second Vatican Council. We are now to use the goods of this world with care, healing them, transforming them, letting them be what God intended them to be, and enjoying them to the glory of God. Everything is directed to God. John was ahead of his time. He never used the vocabulary of integration, but he certainly had the concept. We must integrate all of life in our total dedication to God. Never making objects or even religious devotions ends in themselves, we must organize our lives so that every aspect joins together in one unified self gift to God, creating an emptiness for God to fill. When we read of attachment and detachment in John, we should understand total integration.

The soul. John describes the stanzas of the poem the "Dark Night" simply as "stanzas of the soul." Throughout the commentary, as in other books, John speaks about the actions and involvement of the soul. First of all, this should not be viewed as some distinction between soul and body, with the preference being given to the soul to the neglect of the body. This is not John's way of viewing things; he evidences no sign of dualism in his thought or writings. John uses "soul" as we use "person."

There is much to be said for the idea that the soul is John himself, and that the writings reflect an autobiographical focus. John has already made this journey and can speak of what he has experienced. "And because the soul in this way concentrates only on God, God receives praise and exaltation in manifesting to it his excellence and grandeur" (A.3. 32.2).

John's teachings are gifts to the nuns and friars of the reform and also to many others, clergy, religious, and laity who have been influenced by his works. There is, however, a further way in which John's writings are a gift, and that is that he is a gift to the Church—he is a doctor of the Church. So, it is possible to understand the soul as the soul of the Church, and John is calling the Church to a shared reform and renewal. So, John can link together the goal of the spiritual journey, the soul, and the Church in a shared experience. "For a little of this pure love is more precious to God and the soul and more beneficial to the Church, even though it seems one is doing nothing, than all these other works put together" (C. 29.2).

However, perhaps the simplest way to understand soul is to think that it is John's term for "person," the interested and dedicated reader. He draws each reader into the dynamism of the journey. So, the reader is called to happiness in taking the road of the dark night, the reader departs from love of both self and all things, the reader is gradually drawn out of the stage of beginners to enter the dark night (see N.1. Explanation).

When reading John and seeing his focus on the soul, it possibly refers to himself, it implies his call to the whole Church, and it especially reflects his hope that each reader will take all this as a personal call directed to himself or herself.

Always endeavor to choose that which is most difficult. We all know people who immerse themselves in religious practices but never seem to get any closer to God than they ever were. Of course God chooses when and how to bestow divine life. Nevertheless, we often cannot help but feel that some people spend lots of time on secondary religious practices and devotions—not to say total religious trivia, and yet they get nowhere particular on the spiritual journey and even retain the same faults and failings they always had. They accumulate practices from religions' various menus but never get to the heart of the journey to loving union with God. John decided early in life that if a person wants to get to the top of the mountain then he or she must be willing to make hard decisions.

I have known many people who worked in administration and were forever making lots of decisions on secondary issues but never managed to face up to the few major hard decisions that could transform an organization. Likewise, in various religious groups, their leaders leave unanswered the same critical issues that have plagued them for decades, but seem too difficult to deal with. Also in the spiritual life we must face up to the overriding difficult decisions, and if we do, then the secondary needs will generally take care of themselves.

John's advice that we always endeavor to choose to deal with that which is most difficult is wise advice that can speed up the process of transformation. We must develop a habit of mind that enables us to choose wisely, we need to be always suspicious of our motivations, and we strive to move away from self-centeredness. In John's diagram of Mount Carmel those people who cannot make the hard decisions but immerse themselves in secondary ones are they who walk with religious enthusiasm through the valley of earthly goods and the valley of heavenly goods—the ways of the imperfect spirit. For those who have the courage to climb by way of the narrow center path, he gives them seven pieces of advice— nothing, nothing, nothing, nothing, nothing, nothing, and nothing—because God is no-thing. It is not that John is negative towards life and its values. He does urge that all life evidence a single-minded pursuit of God with no secondary goals that digress from one's commitment. He insists that we make hard decisions for God and loving union and nothing else, nothing that leads us astray, nothing that distracts, nothing that is merely partial, nothing that weakens our pursuit, and so on.

When a person always chooses that which is most difficult, in other words has a habit of not just choosing based on pleasure-pain motives, there are consequences to face. Such a person is not directly seeking the consequences but is willing to pay the price for what he or she seeks. When one makes the hard decisions of the spiritual life one may be faced with opposition, suffering, hatred, poverty, and the loss of everything one held dear. For example, having or not having possessions is not significant in itself for the spiritual journey; Catalina had nothing, Doña Ana de Peñalosa had much. Both chose the single pursuit of God, with all the hard decisions that implied, and they paid the price. John was faithful to his commitment to God and accepted the consequences in his cruel imprisonment. He did not seek suffering but tried to joyfully accept it in faith as a consequence of making hard decisions. It is time for all of us to listen to some sound advice: endeavor to always choose that which is most difficult, that which directs life towards God.

Remember A Few Practical Suggestions for Reading John's Works

Avoid entering John's works with prejudice. We cannot allow John's forms of expression to distract us from the content. Anyone reading John today is faced with the usual problems one meets when dealing with works from another period of history. Many of John's expressions may seem unusual, even unacceptable, to contemporary readers. His approach to Scripture is not historical-critical and thus different than our own today, and he lacks any explicit liturgical focus in his system. His emphasis on suffering may seem exaggerated, and many will be put off by his seemingly negative approach to the world and its values. Referring to John as "doctor de las nadas" is so inaccurate, for he is truly "doctor de los todos"—and wants our desires to be greater than they are. He sought everything of which the human person is capable, and he was simply willing to do and undergo whatever was necessary for union with God. John was one of the most balanced personalities of religious, spiritual, and mystical history. He was willing to accept the purification and "cost" for what he desired to receive from God. We must not enter the works with prejudice but rather appreciate that his presentation is culturally restricted. Our challenge is to be aware that the basic content and dynamic of the spiritual life are perennially challenging. There will be times when John might put us off with his language and ideas. But looking at the total picture of the spiritual life that he presents, we must acknowledge that he is probably correct in his vision. Thus, we separate his culturally restricted presentation from the perennial values of the realities of the spiritual life that he presents.

Read John's writings directly, often, and reflectively. If we wish to understand John's contemporary challenge, then we should read his works directly, frequently, and reflectively. Unfortunately, many Christians have had bad initial experiences of John through misinterpretations of him and his works. It is now crucial that readers lay aside any former negative feelings and simply be open to John's influence, enthusiasm, and challenge. We should also read those parts of John's works that describe stages in the spiritual life that we have not attained, for these too can challenge us and excite us, motivating us for the future. When I read John I find it necessary to be in reflection and stillness; to have what the early spiritual writers called the prayer of the body. John is not easy, and reading him needs reflection, prayerfulness, and interiority. John insists we need purification to make the journey through the nights; we also need purification to read John's works with spiritual benefit. So we should approach John with humility and hope.

Enter into dialogue with John. When we read John we should follow the central argument in his presentation, that clear line of the vital process he wishes to describe. He frequently digresses, gives clarifications that we may not find helpful, and repeats ideas a lot. We must keep focused on the major issues he is addressing and leave aside any digression. I prefer to listen to John rather than read him, so that he is talking to me; and I enter into dialogue with enthusiasm. We must listen attentively to John, aware that it is a privilege to hear what he has to say, and we must try to be worthy. It is important to approach John's writings with a sense of need, emptiness, and longing to know the journey of life. Reading John of the Cross's writings is an invitation, and we will need perseverance. Many people, even dedicated ones, need to acknowledge that the system on which they base their spiritual lives simply does not work and is shallow. They can read what they like and think what they like, but sooner or later they know that John of the Cross is right. All their defense mechanisms need to be laid aside, and they must face the reality that John's system of the spiritual life is the solid, tried, and true one that leads a person to God.

Appreciate the unique focus and message of each work. We should give ourselves totally to whichever work we are reading. *The Ascent of Mount Carmel* is different than the *Spiritual Canticle*; the former presents the journey of faith, the latter the journey of love. Each work has its own point of view, and we must follow that and not take the view of one into another. However, by the time John writes his major works he has a very clear understanding of the entire systematization of the spiritual life. Whichever book we read we can see the essential flow of the stages of the spiritual life. We should immerse ourselves in the book we choose to read, giving ourselves totally to the challenge with confidence and hope. Dabbling with interest is not the same as total immersion.

Always remember the central significance of the poems. The poems are the most faithful living expression of John's mystical experience. Moreover, the language of poetry is suggestive and can evoke different reactions at different times in our lives or in different people. Once you have read his major works and understood the general flow of the system you can go back to the poems and they remind you of his major insights. Troubadours, storytellers, and poets are not as important in some cultures as they used to be, but they touch a level of consciousness that others never do.

Establish your own personal order for reading John's works. Some people find that the *Ascent of Mount Carmel* and the *Dark of the Soul* are too hard to begin with. So, many consider that the *Spiritual Canticle* is a good way to begin. Others find that the shorter writings of John can act as a general introduction to the rest of his works. I have always chosen the *Ascent* and the *Dark Night* as the first books I wanted to read because I always feel that we must read the *Spiritual Canticle* and the *Living Flame of Love* with awareness of John's total vision, lest his journey of love be misinterpreted. Love is hard and demanding.

Above all remember to interpret John's message for today. We do not read John merely to gain clearer understanding of how people understood discipleship in the sixteenth century, but to gain insight into what Christian commitment means for us in our own time and place. So, we need to read John with an eye on our own situations—personal, ecclesial, and societal. Some spiritualities come and go, and it is appropriate that some die as they become irrelevant to changed situations. John is as relevant today, or maybe more relevant, than ever, but we must interpret his language, concepts, dynamic development, and insights to our own situations. I hope other readers can approach John of the Cross with the enthusiasm I feel. I am not a Carmelite; in fact I have never known a single Carmelite other than students, readers of my books, and participants in my workshops. But John has become the most important spiritual guide of my life. I approach him with respect, reverence, and enthusiasm—aware of course that his impact on me can always become one of the obstacles he would want me to reject. He is a giant of mystical theology, prayer, and spiritual direction.

Enthusiasm for John Of The Cross

If you read John of the Cross be ready to encounter the exceptional. He is an exceptional person; humane, gentle, and serene, but challenging and rigorous in commitment. He is frugal, but extravagant to the sick and the poor. He is patient and long suffering in his trials, but strong-minded in business matters, in tolerating the brutal treatment in prison, in dealing with conflicting ecclesiastical power structures. John speaks of the dark night, but his own life also included the lighter side in music, art, sculpture, dance and friendship. He speaks of darkness but has a taste and love for beauty (see C. 36.5) and light. He is reserved, but can dance and sing in community. He is a lover of solitude who can foster easy companionship. He delights in seclusion but dedicates himself to pastoral ministry and outreach.

John is also remarkable in his analytical skills, his discernment, and guidance of others. John is quite unique. No one can confuse his style with any other writer. His style and method indicate a strong personality. He received outstanding academic training at Salamanca, was thoroughly grounded in Aristotelian-Thomistic philosophy and theology, and benefitted from the geographical and cultural heritage of Castile and Andalusia. John was a great communicator, poet, writer, spiritual director, and administrator.

Above all John was a person of integrity and wholeness; a man with a unified personality. He was single-minded and single-hearted in his pursuit of union with God. A lot of people dedicate themselves to God but they never get beyond their initial commitment. John did because he was always open to growth and willing to take the whole costly journey to God. John likes to set a clear direction and then do what needs to be done to get there.

When I read John I feel attracted to his spiritual independence. He tells it like it is and leaves the reader to read and be influenced by God. John is single-minded but avoids dogmatizing his own views. His teachings are very demanding, but they present us with the demands of love and challenge us to love nothing but what God loves. The *Dark Night* may well be his most demanding work but it evidences an excitement and enthusiasm that exceed his other works. He has an absolute conviction of divine transcendence, he knows the way to God, and cannot wait to tell the reader how to get there.

When we read John's works we should do so with simplicity of spirit, striving to participate in the circle of love he creates. We respect the love that inspires him and seek to share it. We should develop mutual friendship with him, as he endeavors to establish a communion between himself and the reader. At the same time we will need a willingness to be empty, receptive, and eager to learn. If we do, there is a chance he will carry us along in the direction he pursues. It is clear he is forceful and energetic, and longs for our growth. As we read the *Dark Night*, we remember that through all his hardships John maintained his values, strove after unchanging goals, and never became like his persecutors nor succumbed to bitterness He came through it all an extraordinary human being, who achieved his goals without trampling on anyone, without abusing the power religion gives, and without reducing the ideals he had maintained from his youth.

CHAPTER FOUR
UNDERSTANDING THE
BOOK OF THE DARK
NIGHT

General Comments

John's own experience of the dark night during the time spent in the Toledo prison unquestionably forms the background to this book. Abandoned, in poverty, emptiness, rejection, and pain, he reaffirms his faith in the absolute otherness of God: "For I know well the spring that flows and runs." This poem is a beautiful description of the intimate life of the Trinity and of how God shares that life with us. John entitled the poem "A song of the soul which delights in knowing God by faith." This mysterious poem has a beauty all its own; a remarkable summary of John's faith that God is always "calling out to creatures," and they can "satisfy their thirst" for life in God alone. However, believers make every step of the journey to God "although it is night." There is no getting away from the realization that we get where we long to be only "because it is night." In the darkness of his prison cell, John experienced the awesome beauty of God, an experience that took hold of him and swept him off his feet, as he felt transformed in God's beauty (see the extraordinary paragraphs, C. 36.5 and 11.10).

It is remarkable in its own way to recall that John's dark night in Toledo produced his greatest love poem, the *Spiritual Canticle,* also the most extraordinary synthesis of God's love for humanity described in the "Romances," and also the haunting reaffirmation of faith and love in the poem mentioned already. John's darkness produced the love, beauty, and gratitude that characterize profound faith. Darkness led to illumination, and the pain of purifying contemplation transformed his entire life.

Some writers have thought that John wrote the poem, "One Dark Night," while in prison, but that is most unlikely. Rather, he probably wrote the poem in El Calvario or Beas, certainly in light of the prison experience (see A.1. 15.1 and N.2. 14.1) and most likely within a year of that experience. There is an extraordinary power in the poem, "One Dark Night." Perhaps, more than any other mystic, John gave beautiful poetic expression to his experience. This poem is real; it does not come from someone's imagination, but rather it is an expression of John's personal experience. However, it is an experience that many men and women undergo, and they find John's articulation touches them, clearly to a lesser degree, but genuinely and authentically. We have all encountered darkness and emptiness, and when we read John's mystical language it becomes suggestive of our own struggles and searches. Of course, one can read "One Dark Night" at different times in life, and each time it means something different as our own experiences deepen, the darkness becomes more painful, and the illumination more transforming.

John refers to the poem as "Songs of the soul that rejoices in having reached . . . union with God, by the path of spiritual negation." So, the poem is written after one has come through this journey of the dark night. There are eight stanzas which highlight the various stages in the journey from the dark night, glad night, guiding night, night more lovely than the dawn, to a night that has united the Lover with his beloved. There are three tempos or rhythms to the poem. The first three stanzas—which are the ones John comments on in detail—are quiet and calming, "my house being now all stilled." With the fourth stanza we are introduced to a new exciting tempo, continued in the fifth, an excitement of search, encounter, and transformation. The last three stanzas speak of peaceful satisfaction, shared love, and loving abandonment. All this takes place in darkness. Book One of the *Dark Night* comments on the first stanza, focusing on the nature of the passive night of sense. Book Two utilizes stanza one to describe the passive night of spirit, stanza two to highlight the various characteristics of contemplation during the passive night of spirit, and stanza three to outline the properties of the passive night of spirit.

While in Beas John began his commentary on the *Ascent* (around 1581-85), so the poem "One Dark Night" was already written. John wrote the commentary on the *Dark Night* while in Granada (1582-85). In fact Fr. Jeronimo de San José claimed he saw John write the *Dark Night* while in Granada.[7] As we have seen, the commentary on the *Dark Night* should be viewed as an integral part of the *Ascent-Dark Night*, in fact, as the fourth book. The prologue to the *Ascent* that describes John's approach to his work, his reasons for writing, the problems he hopes to address, and his presumed audience, is equally valid as a general introduction to the *Dark Night*. When John wrote this important work the only divisions he had were those dependent on the commentary on the stanzas. The first editor of John's works, P. Salabanca, in 1618, divided the *Dark Night* into two books and into fourteen and twenty-five chapters respectively. The division into two books was based on John's understanding as he states, "It is time to begin our treatise on the second night" (N.1. 14.6). So, the *Dark Night* has two main sections: the passive night of the senses (Book I) and the passive night of spirit (Book II). *The Dark Night* is not like the *Spiritual Canticle*, neatly divided into verses with commentary. Rather, *Dark Night* has long sections, goes back and forth in repetition, and becomes quite complicated in places. So, the 1618 editor's division into chapters has proved useful.

This current book is a study-guide to the *Dark Night*, which is itself a study-guide to the poem as John indicates in the title. In the *Dark Night* John describes the rigorous transformation by God of a person who is open, ready, and willing to receive and to respond to this call. It is an uncompromising battle against selfishness to prepare one for union with God. It is strange that John's relentless pursuit of God through purification of selfishness and false attachments has been criticized. We find it acceptable that an athlete train, run, lift weights, and put his body to its limits to prepare for one hour of football a week. Or, that a young woman diet, exercise, deny herself food, and do everything a personal trainer demands in order to keep herself thin enough and in shape to be a model. However, many think John of the Cross is extreme in doing what he does in order to pursue union in love with God. What has happened to our priorities?

In writing the *Dark Night*, John gives helpful advice, suggests stages of growth that can be helpful in theology and spiritual direction, but insists they are fluid and very individual. "Not everyone undergoes this in the same way" (N.1. 14.5). "It is better to explain the utterances of love in their broadest sense so that each one may derive profit from them according to the mode and capacity of one's own spirit" (C. Prologue.2). The *Dark Night* does not refer much to the stages of life, giving an initial reaction that the *Dark Night* refers only to what happens in contemplation. But, this is not so. The *Dark Night* affects every aspect of life. Moreover, the journey of the *Dark Night* is not spiritual purification or endurance alone, but a love-motivated journey to union. So, some disciples of John suggest reading the *Spiritual Canticle* before the *Dark Night*, so that the *Dark Night* can be understood as a journey of love.

Nevertheless, the *Dark Night* is a carefully crafted presentation of the need for total purification of everything that is not God-directed. "The reason he says all this is to explain that nothing but what belongs to the service of God should be the object of our joy. Any other joy would be vain and worthless, for joy that is out of harmony with God is of no value to the soul" (A.3. 18.6). John constantly calls us to search for total commitment to union with God in love (todo), and to be willing to make the sacrifices necessary (nada) to gain the All. This is not primarily a journey of denial but of love and courageous affirmation of one's true self—the discovery of who God is calling one to be.

An Outline of the *Dark Night*

The Ascent of Mount Carmel (Also valid as an introduction to the *Dark Night*)
    Explanation.
    Theme.
    Poem.
    Prologue: John's approach to this work.
        His reasons for writing.
        The problems he hopes to address.
        Some advice for readers.
        His intended audience.

- -

The Dark Night of the Soul.
Introduction: The book focuses on the way to union with God through love.

Book One: The Passive Night of the Senses.
Explanation: This book describes the method used during the journey to God.

Preliminary considerations to the passive night of sense.
1. A description of beginners' imperfections and their need of the dark night.

Characteristics and imperfections of beginners exemplified in the seven deadly sins.
2. Spiritual pride.
3. Spiritual avarice.
4. Spiritual lust.
5. Imperfections of anger.
6. Imperfections of spiritual gluttony.
7. Imperfections of spiritual envy and spiritual sloth.

The dark night of contemplation—nature, signs, and fruits.
8. An explanation of the passive night of senses (a commentary on verse 1 of stanza 1).
9. Signs for recognizing the passive night of the senses.
10. Conduct required of people in this dark night of the senses.
11. Early experiences of love in the dark night.Some benefits of the passive night of sense.
12. Other benefits, especially the development of virtues.

The varied length and experience of the passive night of sense (a commentary on the last verse of the first stanza).
13. Duration and accompanying trials of the passive night of sense.

Book Two: The Passive Night of Spirit.
Preliminary considerations to the passive night of spirit: the proficients' experience.
1. A description of the experience of proficients.
2. Some imperfections and dangers of proficients.
3. Real purification is the work of the spirit.

The nature of the dark night of contemplation, the passive night of spirit (a commentary on the first stanza).

4. Need of the passive night of spirit.
5. Nature of the passive night of spirit.
6. Afflictions suffered in the passive night of spirit (awareness of one's own misery, poverty, and emptiness).
7. Other afflictions of the passive night of spirit (remembrance of past evils, blessings, losses).
8. Further afflictions of the passive night of spirit (purification of intellect, memory, and will).
9. The dark night gives light—positive effects of the Dark Night.
10. An example of purification: simile of a log consumed by the fire.

The fruits of the passive night of spirit.

11. The enkindling of love.
12. The enkindling purifies and cleanses and also illumines.
13. Other delightful effects.
14. Explanation of the last three verses of the first stanza

Characteristics of contemplation in the passive night of spirit (Description of the Passive Night of Spirit).

15. An explanation of the second stanza.
16. The security of the Dark Night.
17. The secrecy of the Dark Night.
18. Contemplation--the secret wisdom is a ladder with ten steps.
19. The first five steps of the ladder.
20. The remaining five steps.
21. "The disguise and colors of the soul.
22. "Ah! The sheer grace" of the Dark Night.
23. "In concealment"—the hiding places of the soul in the Spirit from evil.
24. "My house being now all stilled"—the possession of love in divine union.

The three properties of the passive night of spirit.
25. An explanation of stanza three of the three good properties of the Dark Night.

The Dynamism of the Spiritual Life

Possible stages in development.

In his presentation of the dynamic development of the spiritual life John was originally considered a disciple of Pseudo-Dyonisius the Areopagite, who divided the spiritual life into three main stages: beginners, proficients, and perfect, corresponding to the purgative, illuminative, and unitive periods of life. Writers dependent on this insight generally considered the three stages to be important but rarely gave any importance to the transitions from one to the other.

John's own experience together with extensive knowledge gained through spiritual direction gave him better insight into the stages than anyone prior to him. To the traditional three-fold division John highlights the two crucial transitions. John knew from his own experience of night that crises can be moments of grace and progress, and he called the two transitions the night of sense and the night of spirit. The former was the transition to contemplation, and the latter the decisive moment of life as the complete trusting abandonment to God. The three stages of prior understandings remain and the second becomes a plateau of rest between the nights.

Thus, the nights become so important that John describes the entire journey to God as a dark night. "The darkness and trials, spiritual and temporal, that fortunate souls ordinarily undergo on their way to the high state of perfection are so numerous and profound that human science cannot understand them adequately. Nor does experience of them equip one to explain them. Only those who suffer them will know what this experience is like, but they won't be able to describe it" (A. Prologue.1). Dedicated people who have started the journey come to a point where they advance no more. The problem is clear to John; for one reason or another they do not abandon themselves to God's guidance and enter the dark night. "[A] soul must ordinarily pass through two principal kinds of nights. . . . The first night or purgation . . . concerns the sensory part of the soul. The second night. . . concerns the spiritual part" (A.1. 1.1-2). The first night occurs when beginners transition to contemplation, the second night occurs when proficients move to union. The dark night is an experience of purification, but the motivation for entering it is love. There are three reasons for calling this journey a dark night. The point of departure is a commitment to the denial of one's appetites and to a rejection of self-centeredness and gratification as motives in life which is a dark experience of privation for the senses. The means or way to union is faith which is a dark unknowing experience for the intellect. The point of arrival is God who is an incomprehensible mystery—a dark night to any person in this life (see A.1. 2.1).

The two nights, of sense and of spirit, have two parts, one active and the other passive. The active is a time of ascetical preparation and a deliberate practice of the three theological virtues. The latter is the beginning of contemplation and the inflow of God's transforming action by means of the three theological virtues. Some writers see the active night of sense to be first, followed by the passive night of sense which is the entry into contemplation. However, the active night of sense will continue through contemplation.[8] In fact, the illumination of contemplation throws further light on more unconscious levels that need active purification. The active night of sense is the effort to remove faults and sins one can see, but there are lots of faults one cannot see without God's illumination in contemplation. Some have periods of rest after which comes the active night of spirit, followed by the passive night of spirit.

Others see the active night of sense as first, followed by the active night of spirit along with the passive night of sense as two parts of the same experience. Then the passive night of spirit follows. However, the experiences of active night of spirit and passive night of sense continue to surface and purify even during any respite or plateau periods.

Reflections: In our spiritual journey we enter the thick darkness where we encounter God (Ex 20:21) and God gradually turns our darkness into light (Is 42:16). The journey through the passive nights is entirely in the hands of God. "In the first place it should be known that if anyone is seeking God, the Beloved is seeking that person much more" (F. 3.28). The point of departure is not our efforts but a loving God who is drawing us through the darkness to the light (N.1. 1.1; N.2. 1.1).

This is a journey that consists in the pursuit of no thing, a new discipline that the soul imposes on itself or allows and undergoes in God. John speaks of the nothingness of all creation in comparison with God and of all created and spiritual things as means to union with God. It is not that he despises any of them but that he sees everything as nothing in relation to God (N.1. 4.4-7). This can be a disconcerting aspect of John's teaching unless we constantly remember his goal of everything re-found in God; through poverty and nakedness in God we possess all (see "Prayer of a soul taken with love").

Poverty and negation, or mortification of voluntary, habitual imperfections that move us away from God are means to liberate us from what is false in ourselves, in our world, and in our understanding of God (A.1. 11). This becomes a spiritual empowerment and gives us the freedom to choose the good, to eliminate all that is not of God, and to pursue eagerly only what is of God. Thus, we become dry and ready to be set on fire. "For to love is to labor to divest and deprive oneself for God of all that is not God" (A.2. 5.7).

The active night of sense.

Beginners are good people, resolutely dedicated to God, whose lives are characterized by lots of time given to prayer, fervor in religious practices, and mortification. Their prayer is meditation. So the first step on this journey, for John the point of departure, is the dark night of the sense (see A.1. 2.1), which is equivalent to the mortification of the appetites, the removal of the gratification or pleasure found in sense objects or spiritual things that used to lead to God. This is a period of active ascetical choice and commitment; the focus is not merely on prayer and devotions but on a program of self-discipline, correction of faults, living out one's priorities, and a single-minded dedication to God. Clinging to objects, practices, notions, experiences, and causes of religion that once helped us on our journey to God becomes an obstacle to encountering God who is not like any object of sense no matter how spiritual. "Only those who set aside their own knowledge and walk in God's service like unlearned children receive wisdom from God. . . . Accordingly, to reach union with the wisdom of God a person must advance by unknowing rather than by knowing" (A.1. 4.5). When a person has an inordinate attachment to an object of sense—physical or spiritual—absolutizing it, and seeing it as an end in itself, such a person can never give self totally to God, and furthermore such attachment wearies, torments, darkens, defiles, and weakens one's single-minded commitment to God (see A.1. 3.1; A.1. 4.1). "Consequently, the light of divine union cannot be established in the soul until these affections are eradicated" (A.1. 4.2). Beginners make active efforts to correct these failings—all part of a diligent preparation to give oneself more fully to God.

"It should be understood. . . that a person ordinarily enters this night of sense in two ways: active and passive" (A.1. 13.1). The former refers to what a person does with his or her own efforts, whereas the latter refers to what God accomplishes in the person who is open and receptive. John gives several pieces of advice to one who wishes to actively contribute to the purification implied in the active night of sense. John seeks a re-education of sense not a putting to death of sense (mortification). He has little interest in penance for its own sake (see A.1. 8.4). John's advice is clear and practical. First, concentrate on bringing life in conformity with Christ's, having a greater love of Christ than anything else. The key element for entering the nights is love of Christ and desire to imitate him and to seek union that is a union of likeness in love. "First, have a habitual desire to imitate Christ in all your deeds by bringing your life in conformity with his" (A.1. 13.3). Second, renounce any sensory satisfaction that is not exclusively for the honor and glory of God. Third, bring the four natural passions in harmony and peace by choosing to do that which is most difficult, the removal of habitual, voluntary imperfections that lead one away from God. Fourth, view yourself honestly in light of your failings and be ready to hear of unconscious failings. In addition to these concrete recommendations, John advises readers to put into practice the suggestions he gave on the sketch of Mount Carmel. John approaches the purification of the night of sense with his usual sense of balance and appreciation of human responsiveness. "[T]he appetites are not all equally detrimental, nor are all equally a hindrance to the soul. . . . to mortify them entirely is impossible in this life. . . they are not such a hindrance as to prevent one from attaining divine union" (A.1. 11.2).

Reflections: Nowadays, beginners would probably want to change religious and liturgical practices to suit their own temperament, evidence an inability to deny themselves something through love, lack an ability to really choose, show some inconsistency in their duties, and consider the practices of the externals of faith as childish. Instead of vocal prayer or meditation their prayer would probably be a simple desire to just be quiet in the presence of God.

John's advice for today in approaching the active night of sense could possibly be: imitate Christ in the daily decisions of life; practice moderation in the exercise of external senses, avoid excesses of novelty, new sensations, and experiences; without personal display and without inconveniencing others, be suspicious of the easy and comfortable, seek what is the most difficult especially regarding charity to others; always choosing what is the most loving thing to do; and control pride in all its manifestations.

The active night of sense is really a re-education of sense, a strengthening of sense in its correct use in all external activities and actions of touch, taste, looking, words, body, and activity of passions. It is God's way of preparing a person for the life of the Spirit.

The active night of spirit.

It is easy to think we are burdened in our journey to God by pleasures and satisfactions of sense. But we are also burdened by what we know, what we remember, and what we love, and also by how we know, remember, and love. These spiritual faculties (intellect-knowing, memory, will-affective power) must be purified if we are to journey to union with God in love. We might think we know who God is, but we do not, and these false images and knowledge must be purified by faith. We might remember how good God has been to us and use this as a point of departure for our journey, but this is so limiting it destroys who God can be for us—something we can only grasp through a purification by hope. We might even strive to love God in our own way, with enthusiasm and dedication, but we thus make God in our own image and likeness, and we have to find a new way of loving which only comes through the purification of charity. This part of purification consists in our deliberate efforts to clarify knowledge, memory, and love and desire.

The active night of spirit refers to a process of purification of any satisfaction that comes from the spiritual faculties. It means purifying the intellect in faith, the memory in hope, and the will in charity. "Faith causes darkness and a void in understanding in the intellect, hope begets an emptiness of possessions in the memory, and charity produces the nakedness and emptiness of affection and joy in all that is not God" (A.2. 6.2). John deals with the active night of sense in Book I of the Ascent, the active night of the spirit in faith in Book II, and the active night of the spirit in hope and love in Book III. Accompanying this purification of the spirit by means of the three theological virtues is the move away from meditation and discursive prayer to the preliminaries of recollection for contemplation where an individual lives with a quiet, loving attention to God, abandoning the imagination. When a person can no longer meditate, finds no satisfaction in using his or her imagination, and enjoys remaining alone in loving awareness of God, such a person is ready to move on (see A.2. 13).

Book II of the *Ascent* deals with the night of faith which John sees as the nerve of the spiritual life. "Only by means of faith, in divine light exceeding all understanding, does God manifest himself to the soul. The greater one's faith the closer is one's union with God" (A.2. 9.1). In speaking of faith, John refers both to the mystery and its content (see A.2. 2-3) and to a person's attitudes in accepting faith (see A.2. 4) which is itself a part of the mystery. Faith is a personal acceptance of a personal God. The images we have of God are very important for the whole development of the spiritual life. In fact, the active night of the spirit consists in purifying one's images of God. No natural knowledge can ever be a proximate means of union with God, because it can never conceive him as he is (A.1. 4.7).

Book III of the *Ascent* deals with the active night of the spirit as a process whereby with God's help we purify the memory of false images of God—and all its images, even our most enthusiastic and satisfying, are false because they all fall short of who God can be for us in our hope. Much of our image of God comes from the accumulation of all our good memories of God's interventions in our lives. Memories are discursive and one needs a new kind of insight into God. One of the results of union with God is "forgetfulness of all things since forms and knowledge are gradually being erased from the memory" (A.3. 2.8). Consequently, "God now possesses the faculties as their complete lord, because of their transformation in him. And consequently it is he who divinely moves and commands them according to his divine spirit and will" (A.3. 2.8). As we let go and detach from memory we enjoy tranquility and peace, and gain freedom from temptations that can come through the memory. The less other objects are possessed by the memory, the more we can possess God in hope.

Book III of the *Ascent* goes on to deal with the rebirth of love through the active night of spirit. The task here is to change some of what we love or are addicted to and how we love, so that the full force of love can be directed to all that is of God (see Deut 6:5). This implies purifying the will (affectivity) from inordinate attachments, those voluntary, habitual imperfections that diminish a single-minded and single-hearted pursuit of the love of God. Loving union is achieved through the will, so one must desire nothing that is alien to God.[9] Here John uses the unusual word "appetites" by which he means generally a tendency to show affection for anything that leads away from God. John is very detailed in listing every kind of appetite or obstacle whether temporal, natural, sensual, moral, supernatural, or spiritual. John seeks a life of total self-surrender in love. "To come to enjoy what you have not you must go by a way where you enjoy not" (A.1. 13.11); and again, "Deny your desires and you will find what your heart longs for" (S. 15). This is the work of bringing one's will and affectivity in conformity with God's will and love. The will is not just the act of choice and will power, but what motivates desire and governs choice. So, the active night of spirit is a process of purification of the spiritual faculties of intellect, memory, and will.[10] It is above all an effort to pursue simplicity and to prepare for receptivity. It is active but non-discursive—active in the exercise of faith, in maintaining oneself at rest, in stillness, in being present to God, in being attentive, in discerning carefully, in concentrating, in receiving loving knowledge (see A.2. 12-14). It is also active in deliberately refraining from pursuing only sensible satisfaction, in accepting grace, in freedom, in perseverance, and in patience (see N.1. 10).

Reflections: Nowadays, these appetites that hinder union are just as likely to be collective as personal, and justified as criteria and convictions rather than seen as clear failures. Thus, burnout, keeping institutions going, sexual dominance by males, lack of women's roles in society, inadequate commitment to social justice, claims to maintain purity of doctrine, are some of the appetites that take people's energy away from love of Christ, but are justified and religiously supported. Likewise, people can love their virtues, good habits, graces, talents, motivations, dedication, projects and causes, religious observances, ceremonies and outward liturgical forms, one's spiritual director—all notable spiritual values that can lead to or away from union with God in love (see A.3. 33-40).

Nowadays, we must continue to purify our image of God. John's warnings against visions, apparitions, private revelations, inadequate discernment by both spiritual director and directee, are equally present today, as religious people get caught up in their favorite devotions, causes, approaches to Church teachings, chosen leaders, media personalities, and gurus. All these attachments must be recognized and put in order.

The passive night of sense.

The passive night of sense consists in a process of purification caused by the illumination of contemplation by which the senses are accommodated to the spirit. This is a passive night that affects beginners who have been dedicated to God for some time and have been involved in the active night of purification of the senses (see A.1. 13.1). Having found satisfaction in the things of God, they have become detached from things that led away from God and are ready for God's further challenges. "God desires to withdraw them from this base manner of loving and lead them on to a higher degree of divine love. And he desires to liberate them from the lowly exercise of the senses and of discursive meditation" (N.1. 8.3). God does this by withdrawing all satisfaction beginners found in their religious devotions. "This change is a surprise to them because everything seems to be functioning in reverse" (N.1. 8.3). Instead of the enjoyment and satisfaction they found in their religious devotions, they now find these same religious practices distasteful, and they feel empty and dissatisfied. Some may respond by working harder than ever at their discursive meditation, but this is not desirable. "They are like someone who turns from what has already been done in order to do it again" (N.1. 10.1). Others show a lot of conscious and unconscious resistance to God's love and illumination, and this needs the purification of actual, habitual, and socially justified sin. We often want ourselves more than we want God, and by clinging to our views of religion we block God out of our lives. John offers three signs that, when simultaneously present, indicate that a person is entering the passive night of sense. First, they cease to find any consolation, either from creatures or from the things of God. Second, they are pained by their own lack of service to God (see N.1. 9; also A.2. 13.2-4; A.2. 14). Third, these persons can no longer meditate as before, and have no desire to apply their imagination to formal discursive meditation, but rather find satisfaction in a quiet, loving attention toward God (A.2. 13.2-4). When these signs are present together, these people should leave meditation without fear and follow the Spirit, for

God is leading them from meditation to contemplation (N.1. 10.1).

So, the passive night of sense marks the transition from meditation to contemplation, the latter being light for the understanding and love for the will. "For contemplation is nothing else than a secret and peaceful and loving inflow of God, which, if not hampered, fires the soul in the spirit of love" (N.1. 10.6). This passive deprivation of sense is accompanied by a new activity of the spirit, a new prayer and a new faith (see A.2. 12.6-7). Since contemplation is incompatible with the images of meditation, one who contemplates cannot meditate and generally does not return to discursive prayer. Moreover, this contemplation can be illuminative and delightful, but also purgative and painful.

In approaching the purification of the passive night of sense, John highlights the typical failures that need purifying, they are now somewhat hidden under the cover of spiritual dedication. So, remarkably, he deals with the seven deadly sins all applied to spiritual weaknesses. Beginners cling to their religious devotions and pietistic supports just as others cling to the sensual versions of the seven deadly sins. Once again, John does not care whether you are attached to power or liturgy, sex or prayer forms, the only thing that matters is the heart's focus on self-satisfaction. All this must be purified through God's interventions in the passive night of sense.

There is unquestionable overlapping between the passive night of sense and the active night of spirit, leading several followers of John to conclude these two stages are intellectually distinct but in practice two aspects of one experience. John gives descriptions of the passive night of sense both in his Book I of the *Dark Night* and Book II of the *Ascent* where he also speaks of the active night of spirit in faith. The activity is not contrary to the passivity but seems a unique supportive readiness for God's interventions, what John calls a "general loving awareness" (A.2. 13.4). In the *Dark Night* he picks up again this active attentiveness when he recommends, ". . . allow the soul to remain in rest and quietude. . . pay no attention to discursive meditation. . . through patience and perseverance in prayer. . . liberate themselves from the impediments and fatigues of ideas and thoughts. . . loving and peaceful attentiveness to God. . . ." (N.1. 10.4). All these recommendations imply active involvement.

Before the active night of spirit is complete there are brief experiences of the darkness to come in the passive purification of spirit (N.2. 1.1). For those who do not respond to these calls for further purification, there follows a road block to further progress.

Reflections: The dark night of sense is only the entrance into that of spirit (see N.1. 14.1). Referring to the active night of spirit, John says, . . . "divine union is not perfected by this night alone" (A.3. 2.14), but only by the passive night of God's purifying interventions. Nowadays, these two aspects of the night are generally experienced together. As the illumination of contemplation emphasizes the roots of faults, the active night must work to remove them.

We must still remind ourselves today that nothing can adequately represent God. Even religion's best efforts still fall short—they are idols in comparison to the reality and wonders of God, for God who is inscrutable does not conform to our images. "However impressive may be one's knowledge or experience of God, that knowledge or experience will have no resemblance to God and amount to very little" (A.2. 4.3).

The passive night of spirit.

The passive night of spirit deals with the transition from proficient to union. John describes in detail the nature of this purification and the pain people experience during this time (see N.2. 4-8). While the night of sense is common and happens to many, "The spiritual night is the lot of very few, those who have been tried and are proficient" (N.1. 8.1). John also points out that God does not normally place a person in the passive night of spirit immediately following that of sense, but rather after many years in the state of proficients with their accompanying serenity and peace (see N.2. 1.1). The description of this night is a profound analysis that shows both John's extensive experience of spiritual direction and his own mystical experience. This struggle for the union of love gives meaning to life. It is the most painful period of the spiritual journey, but the ability to renounce aspects of life that have seemingly been good is a characteristic of authentic love. ". . . [T]he most difficult conquest came about in darkness; but since I was seeking love the leap I made was blind and dark, and I rose so high, so high, that I took the prey" (Poem, "I went out seeking love," verse 2). However, first in this night everything around us falls apart. God no longer seems real, faith loses its challenge, the Church and its teachings seem irrelevant. This dark night becomes a pervasive inner anguish, as a person feels he or she is no longer on firm ground.

Proficients still have actual and habitual imperfections that need to be illumined and purified by the passive night of spirit. With the increased illumination of contemplation an individual feels increased affliction and pain at his or her own unworthiness. Such a person, becoming more aware of the awesome otherness of God, recognizes more accurately his or her own failings. In this darkness caused by illumination one experiences God's absence, feels abandoned and rejected by God, overwhelmed by one's own misery, and it seems one's whole inner self is being torn out. "Although they are aware that they love God, this gives them no consolation, because they think that God does not love them and they are unworthy of his love. Because they see themselves deprived of him and established in their own miseries, they feel they truly bear within themselves every reason for being rejected and abhorred by God" (N.2. 7.7). At this time a person can feel embittered at the loss of past good things and helpless in his or her inability to think of God as was formerly common. In fact, one enters a period where one fears losing God forever. One discovers that God does not act towards us as we thought God would. This shocks us, leaves us empty of previous inadequate knowledge—but this is God's way of teaching us how different God is from what we thought. This night purifies the intellect of all former ways of understanding, the will of all inordinate affections, and the memory of what stirs affliction or disturbance or anticipation, distress, and worry (A.3. 6.3)—thus preparing a person for a new God-given way of knowing in faith, of remembering or anticipating what are greater hopes, and of loving in a new way. Truly, the nights become a deepening of faith, hope, and love; they bring us a new approach to faith, a new mode of hope, and a new vitality and depth of love.

"It remains to be said, then, that even though this happy night darkens the spirit, it does so only to impart light concerning all things; and even though it humbles individuals and reveals their miseries, it does so only to exalt them; and even though it impoverishes and empties them of all possessions and natural affections, it does so only that they may reach out divinely to the enjoyment of all earthly and heavenly things, with a general freedom of spirit in them all" (N.2. 9.1). So, although this night is a progressive surrender to God, it is at core a search of unsatisfied love, more so a continuing pursuit of love (see C. 29.10), and a transformation in love (see C. 12.7).

The passive night of spirit produces an enkindling of love in the person who then searches for God with impatient love. "Although the soul in her progress does not have the support of any particular interior light of the intellect, or any exterior guide. . . , love alone, which at this period burns by soliciting the heart for the Beloved, is what guides and moves her" (N.2. 25.4). Journeying thus, the soul finds security through the dark contemplation that is infused in a person through love. In time the individual begins to feel caught up in this love and to consider all else as insignificant, and comes to experience "the inebriation and courage of love" (N.2. 13.6). John presents ten steps on a ladder of love that leads to union with God. But the goal is not just union for it also implies the total renewal of self. One's humanity is not destroyed in the nights, rather it reaches its full potential. A person then re-finds all values of life in God. What was a dark night becomes "the tranquil night at the time of the rising dawn" (C. 15). John describes the beauty and thrill of this resulting life of union in the *Spiritual Canticle* and the *Living Flame of Love*.

Reflections: In the night of spirit people come face to face with the real, objective picture of life and of themselves; they become profoundly aware of human creatureliness and finiteness, and intensely conscious of humanity's sinfulness. Nowadays, some spiritualities, focusing on human fulfillment, tend to forget where we have come from and the deep seated failures of the human heart. John does not.

In the night of spirit people find themselves in the presence of the utterly awesome otherness of God. Nothing can take the place of God, and most of our efforts, based as they are on our knowledge, experience, memories, and yearnings, are idols—we make God into our own image and likeness. This has to be purified by the dark night of contemplation in which God is active, removing our false images and giving us a truer picture. The dark night teaches us the values of emptiness. Until we are willing to become empty we cannot be filled.

The three most fundamental energies of the soul are the three theological virtues of faith, hope, and love, gifts of God to transform souls and prepare them for union in love with God. In our days we have many means of spiritual growth available to us. However, it is important to remember that the theological virtues are the divine powers given for our growth, and no others compare to these. These three energies of the soul purify love, teaching us how to think about the One we love, how to remember and hope about this One, and how to bring together every dimension of our love as if nothing else matters.

The night of the spirit gives individuals the experience of the horror of being unable to love and of being convinced of being unloved and unlovable. Then it prepares them to love well; to feel the absence of One who is loved, to feel unworthy when in that presence, to long to be with the One who is loved, and to sacrifice everything for his or her loving presence. The night of spirit shows us that when we love someone deeply, we give the Beloved a special place in our mind as knowledge gives way to faith, we give the Beloved a special place in our memories—knowing that lovers hope more than remember, we give the Beloved a special place in our hearts reserved exclusively for this One.

The Dark Night Is Our Only Light

In the book of the *Dark Night* John explains the various stages in the development of the spiritual journey to union in love. John would also be the first to acknowledge that life is more complex than a scheme, and the process described is not completely regular nor the same for everyone. So, while no one wants to impose a scheme on anyone, it is useful to have a general feel for the movement of the spiritual life and key experiences that occur during the progress, and John gives us this with extraordinary clarity. Certainly, there is only one way to God and that is to follow Jesus whose love led him to the cross. The experience of the cross comes in a special way in the nights.

One of John's directees in Granada, with whom he also maintained contact in correspondence, was Doña Juana de Pedraza (L. 11 and 19). She seems to be experiencing some of the "grief, afflictions, and loneliness" of the night. John urges her to be calm and peaceful in her struggles, "they are knocks and rappings at the door of your soul so it might love more." He acknowledges supportively her pain and tells her, "it behooves us not to go without the cross, just as our Beloved did not go without it, even to the death of love." John knows Doña Juana is walking in "these darknesses and voids of spiritual poverty," but he tells her "nothing is failing you." "Do not worry, but be glad." "You were never better off than now," "God does one a great favor when he darkens the faculties and impoverishes the soul." "God is leading you by a road most suitable for you." "Desire no other path than this." Thus, for John the experiences of the dark night are one proof of God's loving interventions in our lives. The night is essential to growth, for growth takes place in transitions and crises. This darkness is a test of love which we must undergo in confidence, patience, and ever deeper faith.

When John's directees rejoice in their satisfying experiences of spiritual life, John worries. When they are immersed in darkness, he rejoices, knowing good things are happening to them. Finding oneself in the night is a sure sign of God's presence to us. It is a time of renunciation and sacrifice, but these are never negative. Rather, they are always choices made in love for a better, risen life of love and union. For John, who understood the journey to God better than most other people, the dark night is an assurance of good things happening. The dark night is our truest, safest, and only light and guide.

CHAPTER FIVE
THE BOOK OF THE
DARK NIGHT BY JOHN OF
THE CROSS - A SUMMARY[1]

Introduction

This book describes the way that leads to union with God through love and some of the characteristics of one who has made this journey. It is a commentary on a poem of eight stanzas; the first two describe the passive night of sense and the passive night of spirit and how one should act during these stages. The remaining stanzas refer to the results obtained from spiritual illumination and union with God through love. The commentary is written from the perspective of one who has already completed the journey and is now looking back.

---

[1] See *Collected Works of St. John of the Cross*, translated by Kieran Kavanaugh, O.C.D., and Ottilio Rodriguez, O.C.D., (Washington, DC: ICS Publications, 1991), "The Dark Night," pp. 351-457. This is an effort to summarize the book of the *Dark Night*; it is about one fifth of the original length. It leaves out asides and duplicate explanations, while faithfully presenting the words and ideas that John writes. There are still some problems with language and concepts that are unusual to contemporary readers. However, in a shorter version it still gives us chance to immerse ourselves in John's context, ideas, and spiritual challenges.

Book One: A Treatise on the Night of the Senses

This book addresses the method used during this journey, namely putting to death attachment to all things and to selfishness. The beginning of the journey is a dark night caused by the purifying results of contemplation which passively reveal deeper levels of selfishness. Those who have made this journey can look back with satisfaction at their good fortune. A person's love of God motivated him or her to make this journey while God's love given in contemplation passively begins to control inordinate passions of sense that can impede the way.

1.   A discussion of the imperfections of beginners.

This book describes the transition from beginners to proficients. Beginners are in a lowly state (e.g. their prayer is meditation), but they should take courage and intensify their desire that God place them in the dark night which will strengthen them in virtue and prepare them for union with God in love. Beginners are already people who have resolutely committed themselves to God's service. God takes care of them and allows them to find increased satisfaction in their spiritual experiences. Beginners increase their spiritual devotions and find lots of satisfaction in them. But this is one of the weaknesses of beginners whose motivation becomes the consolation and satisfaction they experience, while many faults and imperfections remain unchecked, which can only be purified by the dark night. Chapters two to seven show the imperfections of beginners using the seven deadly sins, applied to the spiritual level.

2.   The imperfections resulting from spiritual pride.

Beginners become proud and complacent in their spiritual success, like to speak of spiritual matters to others as if they were teachers not learners, and look down on others who they think have not attained their spiritual growth. As their devotion increases, so too does their pride. They compare themselves to others, blind to their own defects and critical of others' weaknesses. They enjoy public acclaim and seek it, want others to be impressed by them, and are hostile to criticism. They can become consumed with envy of others' holiness, refuse to acknowledge their own failures, and have an intense desire to appear better than they are. These beginners minimize their faults, become discouraged, impatient, and angry at their failings, and long to remove them for the personal satisfaction that would give them. They like to receive praise, but never give it.

All these above weaknesses are present to beginners in varying degrees, with none avoiding at least some of them. However, those beginners who are ready to transition to the next level of spiritual growth see, admit, and reject these weaknesses. They have true self-knowledge, become humble, think better of others than themselves, and seek to emulate the good they appreciate in others. They recognize any satisfaction they experience as a gift of God, but focus more on their own inadequacies than their achievements, for the good they do is always less than they want. They see good in others and weaknesses in themselves, think little of themselves and want others to do so too. In fact, they see any praise they receive as misplaced. These beginners who are ready to move along the road to union are always ready to learn from others. They rejoice when others are praised, feeling rather that they are not serving God as well as they ought. They can readily speak of their own failures, and they seek directors who give little praise and a lot of challenge.

3. Beginners' imperfections of spiritual avarice.

Some beginners are never content with the spirit God gives them. They pursue religious objects, experiences, and satisfaction with a possessiveness of heart. They forget that while people can profit from objects and practices of devotion, it is better to focus on love of God and neighbor.

These beginners will find that it is difficult to purify themselves of attachments without the passive purification of the dark night. But if they do their part, then God will heal them of what they were unable to achieve.

4. Beginners' imperfections of spiritual lust.

A lot of the imperfections of beginners can be called spiritual lust, not because the lust is spiritual but because it proceeds from spiritual things. Sometimes beginners experience impure movements during their spiritual experiences. First, this can be because human nature finds pleasure in spiritual exercises—after all, the spiritual and sensory parts find satisfaction in spiritual renewal. Once the sensory part is purified in the dark night individuals will then receive everything in a spiritual way. Second, the devil can cause these rebellions and impure feelings to cause one to give up prayer, and these can come especially in times of prayer. Third, a person's own fear of such impure feelings can intensify them. The gratification that some beginners find in religious devotions and spiritual things inebriates them, fills them with self-assurance in others' presence, and generates an exaggerated pleasure in others' company. It is true that satisfaction in others' presence can be of spiritual advantage if it leads to love of God, but if the love is inordinate then love of God will diminish. The dark night places these loves in reasonable order, strengthens love of God, and destroys false loves.

5. Beginners' imperfections of anger.

Imperfections of spiritual anger result from the pursuit of spiritual gratification, for when the gratification passes the beginners become irritable, unbearable to others, dejected— all reactions that need to be purified through the dryness of the dark night. Then, through indiscreet zeal these beginners become angry at others' sins and set themselves up as lords of virtue. They also grow angry at their own imperfections in an unhumble impatience, making lots of resolutions but unable to keep them. They lack the patience to wait until God is ready, and this lack of spiritual meekness can only be remedied by the purification of the dark night.

6. Beginners' imperfections of spiritual gluttony.

Few beginners avoid this failure due to the delight they find in their spiritual exercises. Focusing more on the spiritual satisfaction than purity and discretion, they go to extremes in penances, fasts, avoiding the guidance of others as they hide their own weakness and excesses from their spiritual guide. These beginners are unreasonable and imperfect; motivated by the pleasure and satisfaction they find in their penances, they lack submissiveness and any obedience that limits their desire for this accumulation of spiritual practices. They become experts in avoiding obedience and lose an appreciation for it, since they just want to do what they want. They try to make their spiritual director think the way they do, they become sad and testy when they do not get their own way, and they equate serving God with doing what they want.

Such beginners lack appreciation for their own weaknesses and lack fear and awe before the greatness of God. They seek satisfaction in frequent communion, rather than appreciating encounter with God in reverence. What they want is to taste and feel God's presence; but this is not God's way and is a serious imperfection and impurity of faith. This defect carries over to their prayer life, where they pursue satisfaction in the devotion, without which they become disconsolate and think they have achieved nothing. These beginners lose the spirit of true devotion and can even abandon prayer when satisfaction is absent, for they are exclusively motivated by the pleasure they find in their devotions. They would do better to emphasize self-distrust, humility, appreciation of the cross, and perseverance in God's will. While they are always hunting for gratification in the things of God, God seeks to deny them this; that is why they must enter the dark night and be purified of this childish spiritual gluttony. They need spiritual sobriety, temperance, mortification, fear, and submissiveness; they need to learn that perfection is not found in quantity of satisfactions but in knowing how to practice self-denial until God draws them into the dark night.

7. Beginners' imperfections of spiritual envy and spiritual sloth.

These beginners show envy towards the spiritual goods and achievements of others, grieving over others' successes in the spiritual life, resenting when others are praised and they are not. They would do better to be genuinely sad at not having others' virtues, and pleased at others' success. Sloth makes them avoid spiritually challenging exercises and give up practices that do not produce feelings of satisfaction. Seeking such pleasure and delight predominates over self-denial and the pursuit of God's will. They feel an aversion to adapt their will to God's, equating their will and satisfaction with God's will, convinced that what is not their will is not God's will.

Bored with anything that does not produce gratification, they lack the fortitude and effort perfection demands, run away from hardship and the cross, and follow their own whims and satisfactions. The narrow way is saddening and repugnant to them. They cannot actively attain complete mortification of self, so God must accomplish this passively through the dark night; through dryness and darkness God weans them from the imperfections of beginners and moves them to the state of proficients.

8. An exposition of the passive night of sense; an explanation of the first verse of the first stanza.

The dark night is contemplation and has two parts, the passive night of sense and the passive night of spirit; the first purges the senses and accommodates them to the spirit, the latter purifies the spirit and accommodates it and prepares it for union with God through love. The passive night of sense is common and happens to many beginners moving to proficients, the passive night of spirit is for very few proficients on their way to perfect union. The common experience of the passive night of sense is bitter—a lot is written on this. The rare experience of the passive night of spirit is frightful to the spirit—little is written on this.

God desires to free beginners from their selfish ways of loving and from meditation as the only prayer form, and lead them to a different kind of communion free of these imperfections. This transition takes place after beginners have exercised themselves for some time in the practice of virtue and have persevered in meditation and prayer. As a result of some satisfaction gained in prayer, they become detached from the values of the world and gain strength in seeking God. Having controlled their attachment to creatures and endured some dryness and a little oppression, they think they are at their best. It is then that God closes the door on all satisfactions and introduces them to darkness, where they feel lost and do not know which way to turn. Suddenly they can no longer advance in their meditation, experience dryness, and find former spiritual exercises distasteful. This change comes as a surprise to them, for everything seemed to be going very well. This happens usually to recollected beginners who are unlikely to backslide and can more readily reform their unfree appetites for worldly things. Such reform is a prerequisite for entering the dark night of sense, and it occurs soon after beginners start to give themselves seriously to the spiritual life. This experience is common—you can see many beginners suffering this transition, and there are plenty of examples in Scripture.

9. Signs for recognizing this passive night of senses.

The aridities felt in the passive night of sense can equally come from other sources, including lukewarmness, feelings of depression, and physical indispositions, so it is important to recognize the signs that the experience is really coming from the passive night of sense. Here are the three principal signs. First, people entering this night find no satisfaction in the things of God or in creatures either. The purpose of this experience is to dry up and purify the sensory appetite. This dryness is not the result of sin; otherwise these people would seek gratification elsewhere. This first sign could be caused by something other than the passive night of sense, so it is important to also verify the second sign.

The second sign is that individuals turn their memory to God with painful care and because they are aware of their distaste for the things of God think they are not serving God. Clearly this dryness is not the result of laxity or lukewarmness, since the lukewarm are lax and have no solicitude for serving God. Those suffering from dryness resulting from the passive night of sense are solicitous and pained about not serving God as they think they should. The genuine dryness of the passive night of sense can be furthered by other causes including melancholy and depression, but it is still effective. Whereas dryness that comes entirely from causes other than the passive night of sense ends in displeasure and a lack of a desire to serve God. Oppressed by this dryness, the sensory part is cast down but the spirit becomes strong and ready for the service of God.

This dryness results from the fact that God transfers gifts and strength from sense to spirit, thus the spirit tastes the goodness of God but the body tastes nothing and remains dry and empty, whereas the spirit grows stronger and more solicitous about serving God. The spirit does not enjoy these positive experiences immediately but only dryness, since it is still used to sensory satisfaction and is not yet accommodated to receive God's gifts by the dark night. When dryness is the result of the passive night of sense, the spirit gradually feels strength and energy as it gets used to the new taste of God. This is the beginning of contemplation which is dark and dry to the senses. This experience of contemplation as prayer and life—often hidden from the one receiving it—produces a desire to remain alone in quietude without a desire to focus on any particular thought. If souls can remain quiet and unsolicitous, they experience internal nourishment, but they must not force this or they will lose it.

Up to this point souls actively work to purify the faculties, but continuing this work would now be a hindrance. They must leave discursive meditation and enter the state of proficients—active recollection and hopefully contemplation, which is God's work through the passive night through which God binds the interior faculties of intellect, memory, and will, producing a dryness of sense and a satisfaction of spirit. This new found peace is quiet, delicate, solitary, and satisfying, far from the palpable gratifications of beginners.

A third sign that this dryness is a genuine fruit of the passive night of sense is that individuals can no longer meditate nor use their imagination. God no longer communicates through the senses by discursive analysis or synthesis of ideas, but rather through pure spirit in non-discursive contemplation. The exterior and interior senses can no longer attain this, and the imagination is of no use. This third sign confirms that the dryness is exclusively the result of the passive night of sense. If it were otherwise, then people could easily return to their former exercises. In the passive dark night this is no longer possible, there is no going back and the powerlessness to meditate remains. Not everyone walks this road to its conclusion, and God accommodates to their efforts and encourages them when necessary. It is not for us to ask why God does not draw everyone to the life of contemplation.

10. Conduct required of people in this dark night.

Through the experience of aridity God withdraws souls from the life of senses and places them in the life of the spirit. This includes leading them from meditation to contemplation. People suffer much at this time because of the aridity they experience; they feel they have gone astray, lost God's blessings, and even that God has abandoned them. So, they focus on meditation and work harder at it than previously, but they feel an internal reluctance and repugnance and would prefer to dwell quietly in God without using their faculties. If they go back to meditation they can impair God's work, certainly do not profit from their own, and can lose the new found spirit. They should realize that meditation is finished, and they can no longer go back to it.

These people should feel peaceful, knowing that God does not fail those who seek divine life; rather God gives what is needed for this journey to light and love. So, in this night they must pay no further attention to meditation, remain at rest even though they might think they are wasting time or even becoming lax in their lack of effort. This is a time to free themselves from the impediment of too many ideas and thoughts; do not return to meditation or progress will be stopped, rather be content with a loving and peaceful attention to God.

Souls should not worry if they are not using their faculties any more, rather they should rejoice because such use is an obstacle to infused contemplation. Let them peacefully receive contemplation and make room in their spirit for the rekindling of love. After all, contemplation is nothing else except a secret, peaceful, loving inflow of God, and we should not hamper it.

11. Experiences of love; an explanation of three verses of the stanza.

The spirit of love which comes with contemplation does not take hold at first either due to impurities in the sensory part or to the fact that the soul does not understand what is happening and has failed to make space for this new love. However, as the love increases a person becomes aware of being attracted by God's love without fully understanding its source. Eventually, the longing for God's love becomes so intense one feels his or her entire being is drying up in this search.

At first, the soul experiences an habitual care and solicitude for God, accompanied by grief and fear that one is not serving God. God is pleased with this distress and longing, for it is a way contemplation purifies the sensory part, and only when this is done can it enkindle the spirit of love. As one is being prepared for this love only darkness and dryness remain. The purpose of this night into which God introduces the soul is to accommodate, subject, and unite the life of sense to the life of spirit through darkness and the end of meditation. People will eventually appreciate this and enjoy many resulting benefits.

This passive night of sense frees souls from former imperfections such as those resulting from the seven deadly sins, by darkening discursive meditation and producing virtues. This experience of removing any spiritual gratification is hard but produces many blessings. Few endure this and persevere as their inner spirit is despoiled and grounded in faith, but it is a preparation for the passive night of spirit and its pure faith, and will bring greater benefits.

12. Some benefits brought about by this passive night of sense.

Precisely when a person feels he or she is losing former benefits, he or she is getting ready for new ones. The first benefit of this purification of the dark night of contemplation is knowledge of self and one's own misery. Formerly filled with gratification at their own spiritual development, individuals are now empty and made to see their own misery. In dryness, desolation, and darkness one experiences the authentic light of self-knowledge, appreciating his or her own inability to attain anything without God's help.

Many benefits result from this experience of aridity. Souls commune with God more respectfully and courteously, as they lose the misplaced self-assurance they had. Then, with sensory satisfaction quenched, they are free to understand the greatness and majesty of God and the uselessness of the former pleasure they found in the spiritual values of beginners. In this darkness and dryness of contemplation a person rejects former accumulations of self-satisfaction and discovers that in emptiness God can instruct each one in wisdom. So, one does not know God through ideas and meditation but in abandoning these and entering the dark night. This new self-knowledge is the foundation for greater knowledge communicated in the passive night of spirit.

Another benefit resulting from increased self-knowledge is that a person procures spiritual humility, appreciates his or her own weaknesses, and finds a new esteem for the good found in others, being now focused on his or her own failures rather than someone else's. So, such people become more submissive, obedient, attentive to others, and less presumptuous, and as pride is swept away they evidence humility, love of neighbor, and pliability.

13. Other benefits, especially the development of virtues.

First, this dark night of sense leads to a thorough reform of imperfections such as pride, avarice, lust, and gluttony, as a person is liberated from useless sense gratification, passions wither and dry up, and one dwells in spiritual peace and tranquility. Second, a person now bears a habitual remembrance of God, accompanied by a fear of turning back and losing this new knowledge. Third, the soul exercises an integrated commitment to virtues, especially patience, detachment, and fortitude. This brings delight in peace, solicitude for the things of God, and purity of soul. In relation to the other capital sins (anger, envy, and sloth) a person is purified and acquires the opposite virtues. Instead of anger he or she shows meekness and respect for others, instead of envy he or she finds charity to others and a desire to imitate their goodness, instead of sloth a new commitment without the former spiritual gratifications.

In addition to these benefits God gives support, love, and knowledge—all greater than former satisfactions, even though only gradually appreciated. In freedom of spirit people are freed from the power of the three great enemies of the devil, world, and flesh, and are led to acquire the twelve fruits of the Holy Spirit. They now walk with purity in the love of God, with solicitude for the things of God, and with desire only to please God. They discover a new holy fear of their own presumption and self-satisfaction, which in turn preserves and increases virtue. When the person says "my house is now all stilled," he or she knows that God has calmed the negative effects of the four passions, discontinued discursive prayer, purified the sensory part, and welcomes the gift of contemplation.

14. Duration and accompanying trials of the passive night of sense; an explanation of the last verse of the first stanza.

Once the passive night of sense is completed a person goes out to begin the journey along the road of the spirit, the road of the proficients, the illuminative way. Having left aside discursive meditation and active involvement, and surrendered passively to God's activity within, people find that God now nourishes them in a new way. This passive night of sense includes burdensome trials and temptations that can last a long time. The first such trial is the spirit of fornication that assails their senses and even their spirit. Second, people are also tempted to blasphemy. Third, people's senses are darkened with confusion, scruples, and anxiety that leave them disconcerted in ways not unlike what will come in the passive night of spirit. These trials prepare, strengthen, and humble the soul for the union with wisdom that follows.

Not everyone goes through the same trials, nor do they last the same length for everyone. This depends on God's will, the person's need for purification, and the level of love to which God wishes to raise a person. For those who are strong enough the purification can be strong and quick, for others the night can be long, less intense, with moments of refreshment to avoid discouragement. These latter who are coached along by God arrive later at union, some never fully—they remain never fully in the night and never fully out of it. Those who move on to the passive night of spirit have generally endured the passive night of sense for quite a while.

Book Two: A Treatise on the Dark Night of Spirit.

    1.   A description of the proficient's experience.

Generally, God does not place a person in the passive dark night of spirit immediately following that of sense, but a person usually spends many years in the state of proficients, enjoying freedom, satisfaction of spirit, and interior peace. No longer bound by discursive meditation and spiritual concerns of beginners, the individual now enjoys the serenity that comes with loving contemplation. However, total purification is not complete, for the purification of spirit is still lacking. One feels certain needs, aridities, darkness, and conflicts more intensely than in the past. These last for a while but will pass as one returns to serenity—this experience is a brief anticipation of the passive night of spirit. At times God gives some people short experiences of the night followed by serenity. However, those who have the strength and capacity for the prolonged experience can enjoy the delights of God even in the sensory part since that is now purified, although these experiences are reduced and even have negative side effects in unusual religious experiences which indicate the body's inability to cope with the delights of the spirit.

2. Some imperfections and dangers of proficients.

Imperfections of proficients are habitual or actual. Habitual are those imperfections still remaining after the passive night of sense, like deep roots not yet dug out. The purification of senses prepares for that of spirit; the former accommodating senses to the spirit while the latter prepares for union of the spirit with God. Habitual imperfections include the natural affections and dullness that results from sin together with a distracted and inattentive spirit. These too must be illumined, clarified, and recollected by the passive night of spirit.

Actual imperfections occur when people become over-focused on the satisfactions they receive in spiritual communications, beguiled by vain visions and empty prophecies, or drawn by vanity, arrogance, and others' praise. These people become bold in dealing with God and too secure in their new experiences, just at the point when they were ready to make further progress. Too many proficients think this new satisfaction that follows the passive night of sense is more significant than it is, and this unfortunate tendency can only be purified by the passive night of spirit. The blessings that proficients receive are inadequate for union because the lower part of the person still shares in them, an approach that will be lost when a person walks in dark and pure faith in the passive night of spirit.

3. Real purification is the work of the Spirit.

Proficients are attracted by the gratification flowing from their spiritual experiences and this helps them be accommodated and united to the spirit, in such a way that they are ready for what lies ahead. The passive night of senses is just a reformation and bridling of the appetites rather than a full purification. The real purification of the senses begins with the spirit, since all imperfections of the sensory part are rooted in the spirit. In the passive night of spirit both parts are jointly purified; the lower part is purified then strengthened by spiritual support to be strong enough to endure the night ahead.

Since their spirit is not yet purified and illumined, the proficients are lowly and natural in their communication with God and in their activities directed to God. Later, when they reach perfection, union with God, they will do great works. But to get ready, God divests faculties, affections, senses, both spiritual and sensory, interior and exterior; thus, leaving the intellect in darkness, the will in aridity, the memory in emptiness, and the affections in affliction, bitterness, and anguish. When this is done, individuals leave aside the satisfaction found in the initial blessings of proficients, and enter the pure and dark night of contemplation.

4. Passive night of spirit; an explanation of the first stanza.

This stanza refers to contemplative purification, nakedness, poverty of spirit, and describes how one leaves behind the low means of understanding, the feeble way of loving, and the poor and limited method of finding satisfaction in God. No longer experiencing its former supports, rather now in darkness of the intellect, distress of the will, affliction and anguish of the memory, a person is left to journey in darkness to pure faith.

Thus leaving aside one's former way of acting, a person chooses God's way. This implies the annihilation of the faculties, passions, appetites, and affections. Thus, the intellect moves from human, natural knowing to divine wisdom, the will from its lowly manner of loving to divine love with strength and purity of spirit, the memory from the dead past or falsely imagined future to focus on eternal glory. In this way all one's strength and affections are renewed.

5. Nature of the passive night of spirit.

Through infused contemplation which a person receives passively God teaches the perfection of love. This contemplation purifies the person of habitual ignorance and imperfections and leads to illumination. However, we must ask, if this is divine light and illumination why call it a dark night? Because what becomes illumination is at first for each one darkness, affliction, and torment. So, there are two reasons to call it a dark night: the divine wisdom given at this time so exceeds the abilities of a person to receive it so that he or she feels in darkness; the soul feels so unworthy of this illumination that it finds it a painful affliction. Put another way, the clearer divine things are the darker and more hidden they are to a person; the brighter the light the more it hurts an unprepared eye; the supernatural light overwhelms the intellect and leaves one feeling in darkness; thus, weak intellects are blinded and darkened by God's illumination.

So, the unpurified person feels affliction and pain. The first reason for this is that the bright and pure light of God's wisdom hits the sickly, impure, weak eyes of proficients When this happens a person feels unclean and wretched, suffers because it feels God has rejected it, sees its own weaknesses and knows it is unworthy of God and others, feels it will never be worthy to receive future blessings, and sees clearly that of itself it will never possess anything worthwhile again. Thus, this illumination purifies a person by plunging him or her in his or her own miseries. The second reason for this pain is the person's natural, moral, and spiritual weakness before the overwhelming power of God that leads to the feeling of an immense dark load. Oppressed by these burdens, individuals feel the loss of all past favors and sense that what used to give them support has gone. They should know that God's aim is to grant favors and not chastise, but God's gentle hand certainly feels heavy.

6. Other afflictions suffered in this passive night of spirit.

A third kind of pain is that the soul at the sight of its own miseries feels it is being undone by a cruel spiritual death. God's purifying contemplation so absorbs the human spiritual substance that the soul feels it is losing itself, but this tomb of darkness prepares for a spiritual resurrection. In this suffering a person has the conviction that God has abandoned it and cast it into darkness; it experiences God's absence, feels chastised and rejected by God, feels unworthy of God and the object of God's anger. Moreover, such people also feel forsaken and despised by other people, especially their friends.

A fourth kind of pain is that the soul senses his or her own intimate poverty and misery; an emptiness of all that used to please it whether temporal, natural, or spiritual. Such a one now finds himself or herself placed in the midst of miseries of imperfections, aridities, emptiness, and abandonment in darkness. It is in this way that contemplation consumes all the affections and imperfect habits of the individual, leaving him or her feeling oppressed, undone, and in inner torment as the roots of previous imperfections are ripped out.

In fact, at this time, a person feels he or she is approaching the end, as God humbles the soul by tearing out his or her very inner spirit, leaving him or her in a terrible extreme poverty. Only at intervals does a person see this in all its intensity, for if it were continual a person would die, but even so he or she sees hell and perdition through this purification.

7. Other afflictions the will experiences in the dark night.

The afflictions of the will are immense, especially when one remembers past evils, feels uncertain of any remedy, and thinks about past spiritual prosperity. The prophet, Jeremiah, in his *Lamentations*, depicts vividly the trials of one in this purification. We need to have compassion for one who suffers in this night, for he or she feels immense suffering and extreme uncertainty about a remedy. But we should also appreciate that a person is being blessed. However, in desolation such a one finds neither consolation nor support from any source, and feels helpless that there does not seem to be anything he or she can do. This purification is of greater or lesser force, endures a longer or shorter time, until the spirit is humbled, softened, purified, and readied for the union of love.

If this night is to be truly efficacious, it will last for some years, with intervals of illumination, love, and abundant spiritual communication that might even give the soul the thought that the trials are over. But there still remain deeply rooted imperfections that a person does not appreciate during these intervals of reprieve. But the spirit is not yet completely purified and cleansed of sensory affections, and until it is complete these intervals hide the roots of problems that still remain. People who are aware will see that something still remains to be done, for there is an enemy within that is just asleep. It is when a person feels safe and least expects it that the full force of the purification returns giving the impression to the individual that he or she has lost all blessings once again. It now seems to these people that they have virtue but are deprived of God and afflicted; aware they love God but feel God no longer loves them. They know they love God but cannot understand why they have no relief, in fact more affliction; they sense they no longer have nor ever will have anything deserving of God's love, rather they see clearly the reasons for being rejected by the one they love.

8. Other afflictions that trouble a person in this state.

Since the dark night impedes a person's faculties he or she cannot beseech God nor raise his or her mind and affections to God, and even when one manages to pray it does not seem that God hears. But, really this is not a time for prayer but for simply enduring the purification patiently. God is the one working now not the individual. Generally people in this state cannot pray or attend to spiritual matters, and still less to temporal or business matters, for they seem out of it, very forgetful, and unable to concentrate. This night purifies the intellect of its light, the will of its affections, and the memory of discursive knowledge. The brighter the light of contemplation the darker it is to the soul. This contemplation deprives one of all natural affections and apprehensions and leaves a person's spiritual and natural faculties in darkness and emptiness. This happens even though the individual is unaware of it. Thus purified, a person finds a facility in perceiving and penetrating even the deep things of God, and an ease in seeing aspects of his or her own life that need purifying. The soul who has gone through this purification finds no satisfaction in anything in particular, but remains in darkness and emptiness, embracing all things with preparedness.

9. The dark night gives light.

The night of contemplation darkens only to illumine, humbles only to exalt, impoverishes and empties so one can enjoy all earthly and heavenly things. Without purification a person would be unable to experience the joy of the spirit. In fact one attachment would be enough to block this experience. The spirit must be totally purified in order to communicate freely in the fullness of the spirit with divine wisdom and enjoy all things. It is the experience of the dark night that undoes all the lesser ways to prepare for this divine light that transcends all.

The dark night purifies the intellect of its natural object and habitual ways of understanding and this causes great pain. The dark night purifies the will of its former affections and feelings, for the love that is bestowed in divine union exceeds all previous experiences of the will. In dryness and distress a person finds God's grace removes all previous ways of loving. This, too, is painful for the love of union does not naturally belong to the will, but after the expulsion of all former ways of loving the will is transformed. Only when one is set in emptiness and poverty, purified, and stripped of the old self, can one be ready to live the new life of union with God. The memory too needs to be purified of all previous agreeable and peaceful knowledge and become alien to its usual knowledge and experience. Everything seems strange, as one is made a stranger to one's previous knowledge and experiences in order to prepare for divine union.

An individual suffers in the dark night so as to be reborn into the life of the spirit by means of the divine inflow. Likewise, he or she can leave aside all former peace, which was not true peace, for it was both sensory and spiritual, to prepare for a new peace. This passive night of spirit involves many fears, struggles, a sense of being lost, and a feeling that all former blessings have gone. A person suffers greatly at the remembrance of his or her miseries and cries out with profound affliction. Such a person is also filled with doubts and fear that block all sense of hope. The soul feels torn to shreds. The suffering is so great because what lies ahead is great; so great the end, so great the labor and change. However, the contemplation of itself does not produce pain; rather it is a delightful illumination. The pain results from a person's weakness, imperfections, inadequate preparation, and qualities that are contrary to the light. Thus the soul suffers when light illumines his or her life.

10. Explains purification by means of a comparison.

The transforming light of the passive night of spirit has the same effect on a person that the fire has on a log. The fire first dries up the wood, then turns it black sometimes emitting a bad odor, and then by heating and kindling transforms the wood into fire itself. Once the wood is transformed it has no activity or passivity of itself. The wood is dry and dries, is hot and gives off heat, is brilliant and illumines. Contemplation does the same to the person in need of purification. First, the light and wisdom of God prepares a person, second it purifies him or her of all imperfections, third it burns away impurities, and fourth it enkindles in love. Then, fifth the fire of love burns even more intensely, and sixth it helps one become aware of his or her own impurities. Seventh, when the purification returns after a tranquil rest, a person becomes aware that roots of imperfections remain and the purification of God returns to the individual, blinding him or her to all exterior goods and making him or her think all blessings are over.

11. A fruit of the dark night—a vehement passion of divine love.

The enkindling of love resulting from the passive night of spirit is different from that which results from the passive night of sense, for the latter is in the sensory part whereas this is now in the spiritual part. The person in the midst of these trials does not understand anything particular for the intellect is in darkness, but he or she experiences being transformed by a strong divine love. This love is infused, it is more God's action than the person's, and it occurs when all appetites are subjected so that a person is ready to receive this love. God weans the soul of his or her false attachments and recollects, strengthens, and gives the capacity for union in love. Everything about a person is now integrated in love of God with no satisfaction found elsewhere. At first the person becomes aware of the power of this love, but does not possess it, still remaining in darkness and doubt. However, the soul longs for this love and finds no rest. Rather, this suffering unaccompanied by certain hope leads one to intensified anxiety and affliction. Thus, a person longs for God with the desire and anxiety of love. While in this darkness, a person still experiences a certain companionship and interior strength, and when the darkness passes he or she feels alone, empty, and weak.

12. Resemblance of this frightful night to purgatory.

As in purgatory this dark night purges and enkindles, cleanses and illumines by love. Contemplation infuses both love and wisdom in the soul according to its capacity and need and thus removes ignorance. Human beings are impure and feeble and experience darkness, pain, and anguish when this fire of love spiritualizes and refines them through purification. Only then do they become capable of receiving God's inflow of love, and they receive it with distress and longing. This is because they still need purifying and preparing; eventually contemplation will inflame the will and illumine the intellect with knowledge and light. In this experience the will is passive and an individual feels he or she has a fire within because of the new communication of living knowledge. This union of the will and the intellect and the resulting enkindling of love is a delightful experience and a beginning of the experience of union of love. Keep in mind that sometimes the will can love without the intellect understanding, and the intellect can know without the will loving, likewise, the intellect can be in darkness and the will enkindled by the fire of love, or the loving light illumines the intellect but the will remains in dryness.

13. Other delightful effects of the dark night.

The dark night of contemplation at times leads to the burning of the will in love, at other times it illumines the soul communicating mystical knowledge to the intellect, even though the will remains in dryness. Sometimes contemplation acts on intellect and will together—a union more perfect and deeper in quality. Why does the burning of the will precede the understanding of the intellect? Because the intellect cannot receive passive knowledge unless purified, whereas the infusion of love does not directly affect the will which must remain free, but rather affects the appetites of the will. Then one can feel this passion of love even when the will is not totally purified, in fact, the passions even help it experience impassioned love. This thirst of love is different from that experienced in the night of senses. It is far greater and is felt in the higher, spiritual part, even though the sensory part can participate somewhat in the experience. But, the longing of the spirit is greater for it is aware of an immense and incomparable good that it lacks, and intense suffering results.

At this point in the experience of the night the person longs for God and feels he or she has lost God or been abandoned by God. This causes fear, for one could endure this suffering if only he or she knew there was nothing to fear and that God was pleased with his or her efforts. In other words the soul has the love of esteem for God. When later the fire of love comes on top of this esteeming love a person acquires strength, courage, boldness, and longing. This love inebriates a person and fills him or her with courage, for with this love everything seems possible.

At this point an individual rises up and anxiously goes in search of God. This love develops in four phases: 1. Longing love (impatient), 2. Esteeming love (intense, but not passionate), 3. Burning love (passionate), 4. Perfect love (union). Immersed in darkness, a person experiences the absence of God, and is filled with impatient love. Although still feeling unworthy of God, the soul still possesses a bold energy to go and find God and be in union. This love imparts a force to love authentically, and authentic love implies union and so the individual seeks it. However, the intellect is still in darkness and the person continues to see his or her own weaknesses and feels unworthy. As was said above, darkness is not caused by the light but by the individual's imperfections, so at first such a person still only feels darkness and evil. After purification is complete a person sees clearly his or her immense benefits and goods, when the intellect is illumined with supernatural light, the will informed by love, and the memory changed by divine conversion.

14. An explanation of the last three verses of the first stanza.

The enamored soul must leave the security of the house to reach the goal, and so he or she goes out at night when all operations, passions and appetites are asleep, for union is not possible when they are active. In the purification of the dark night, God puts to sleep all these faculties, passions, affections, and appetites, so one can go out to the union of love. What a fortunate experience to be free of the control of senses, such can only be understood by one who has experienced it, and can now understand how the life of the spirit is true freedom.

15. The second stanza.

All the trials of the dark night do not lead to the risk of being lost; rather a person is saved in this dark night. Each one, departing by a living faith, escapes securely and finds greater safety because all its affections are mortified and purified.

16. An explanation of how a person finds security in the dark night.

This dark night of spirit purifies all the sensory and spiritual appetites, binds the imagination so that it cannot do any discursive work, makes the memory cease, the intellect dark, and the will arid and constrained. It is in this darkness that the soul asserts that it walks securely. When the appetites are purified individuals are freed from any error caused by them, liberated from their own evils and from the three great enemies of the world, devil, and flesh. So when a person walks in darkness and emptiness, he or she walks securely, for when his or her evils are impeded, only the good of union with God is imparted to the appetites and faculties. Since these appetites do not have purity and strength or ability to receive these goods in a supernatural way, they must first be darkened, purified of natural ways to lose their human manner of receiving. Thus faculties are prepared for the sublime once the old self dies. Souls themselves can see at this time how little the appetites are distracted, how they are free from vainglory, pride, presumption, false joy, and other evils—thus one avoids going astray and grows in virtue.

The person who now feels darkened, dry, and incapacitated should rejoice, because when God takes a person's hand through the darkness his or her own actions will be purified. One is advancing securely because he or she is getting lost to what was known and tasted, and going by a way neither tasted nor known. People may not understand what is happening to them at this time, but to reach an unknown end along an unknown road travelers cannot guide themselves, they need a guide. Another reason for this sense of security is that a person advances by suffering with the strength God gives, and it is in suffering that virtues are practiced and acquired and the person is purified and made wiser and more cautious.

A further reason why one walks securely in this darkness is that the light of contemplation so absorbs a person that he or she is protected and freed from all that is not God, since God causes one to lose all appetite for anything else. Thus, contemplation brings a person closer to God, in security and loving care. But the closer one comes to God the more he or she feels the pain of weakness and impurity. However, in this dark purification such a person feels protected from harm and increasingly freed of imperfections. Yet another reason for security is God bestows fortitude so that individuals become determined not to commit offenses against God, and not to omit anything that could be of service. In this enkindling of love a person is filled with vigilant care and solicitude for the things of God, paying homage to God and withdrawing appetites from all else.

17. Contemplation is not only dark but is secret.

Dark contemplation is secret because it is mystical theology communicated and infused into a person through love. This infused communication is secret to the intellect and other faculties. The purifying contemplation is secret because the illumination transcends everything sensory and is ineffable, so a person has no way of expressing its meaning, or form an image to explain it to others, even his or her directors. Rather, each one feels quiet, content, aware of God, and convinced all goes well.

This mystical wisdom can also be called secret because it engulfs and hides the person within itself, removed from all else. The individual feels caught up in this love and understands how base all else is. Then, one understands that without special illumination no one could understand these things, and so calls it secret. A final reason this contemplation can be called secret is that it is the way that God guides a person to union through unknowing and ignorance since these experiences are not known humanly. God's illumination causes darkness, and the way to God is hidden and secret, not appreciated while being sought but only when already found.

18. The secret wisdom is also a ladder.

There are many reasons for calling this secret contemplation a ladder. First, a person ascends this ladder to know and possess the goods of heaven. Second, the same steps of a ladder are used for ascent and descent, and this secret contemplation both extols the individual and humiliates him or her. The ordinary procedure in the state of contemplation is that a person never remains in one state, but everything is ascent and descent. On this road there are many ups and downs, after prosperity trial, calm before future penury, abundance and tranquility succeed misery and torment, fast comes before a feast. When the ascending and descending end, a person acquires perfect habits and reaches the top of the ladder in God. So, this contemplation is called a ladder because it is a science of love that illumines and enamors a person elevating him or her step by step to God.

19. The first five of ten steps on the mystical ladder of divine love.

First, a person becomes sick in an advantageous way. He or she becomes sick with love because of his or her sin and loses appetite for all things. This sickness comes as a gift from God, and when a person begins to climb this ladder of contemplation he or she cannot find satisfaction in anything and so moves on to the next step. Second, the person searches unceasingly for God, pays heed to nothing else, and becomes solicitous for God in every aspect of life. So, one convalesces from sickness, searches relentlessly, and then moves on to the next step. Third, this step prompts the individual to good works and gives him or her fervor that it may not fail. It is fear that produces this eagerness, fear of not doing enough, fear one is not responding generously enough. Such are far from presumption and vainglory. Rather, they acquire courage and strength to move to the next step. Fourth, an habitual yet unwearisome suffering is engendered for the beloved. Such people possess lots of energy for self-control, seek no consolation or favors from God, but give all the care to pleasing God at all costs. This pursuit of God in the spirit of suffering is a high step on the ladder and inflames a person's love and desire to move to the next step. Fifth, this step imparts an impatient desire and longing for God, an ardent longing to be united with the beloved without any delay. When this desire is frustrated the longing increases, moving to the next step.

20. The remaining five steps of love.

Sixth, the individual runs swiftly toward God and experiences many signs of God's love. Hope for love invigorates and as charity is increased and purified, he or she can move swiftly. Seventh, God's favor imparts to each one ardent boldness. Such people do not want to wait or retreat, and they obtain from God whatever they ask. Along with this boldness souls must persevere in humility. Eighth, here the person is united to the beloved, satisfying his or her desire for union even though it is not continual. Some get this far but turn back, others rest here for a short time, then move onto the next step. Ninth, one now receives incalculable riches, as the Holy Spirit produces gentle and delightful love—a step of the perfect. Tenth, this last step assimilates the person to God, as he or she is totally purified through love. All that one is becomes like God through participation. These are the ten steps of the secret ladder, although not secret to the soul in the later stages when love reveals a lot through its effects on the soul. On this top step the vision is clear and nothing hidden, or almost nothing, since total union only comes at death.

21. An explanation of "disguised."

People disguise themselves for two reasons, to curry favor with the beloved or to hide from rivals in order to better carry out their plans. The soul, aspiring to win Christ's favor, departs in a disguise that represents his or her affections for the beloved; white for faith, green for hope, and red for charity. The disguise also hides the soul from his or her enemies—devil, world, and flesh. The pure whiteness of faith blinds the intellect against evil and obtains the favor of the beloved. Journeying in faith without the comfort of any intellectual light, one finds that God seems hidden and receives no support from spiritual teachers; rather finding that faith is proved in tribulation.

Green signifies hope that gives courage and strength, and raises a person to things of eternal life. With hope the soul never sets store by anything of this world, but lives only in the hope of eternal life. Thus, such people now concern themselves with nothing save God, and find no satisfaction except in God who satisfies all their hopes. No one can pursue the goal of love without unrelenting hope. Thus, people advance through this dark night and secret night in the disguise of hope, empty of all possessions and supports.

The perfection of the disguise is the red toga of charity which adds elegance to faith and hope and brings one closer to pleasing God. This charity protects each one and strengthens and invigorates all other virtues. Where true love is present, a person leaves aside all other loves and advances to perfect union with God. These three parts of the soul's disguise prepare the faculties for union with God. Faith darkens and empties the intellect, hope empties and withdraws the memory from the created, charity empties and purifies the affections and appetites of the will of everything that is not God—thus leading to union.

22. An explanation of verse three of stanza two.

It is a great grace for any person to undertake this departure, thus liberating self from the influences of the devil, world, and one's own sensuality. In this way a person reaches freedom of spirit, becoming heavenly instead of earthly, divine instead of human. John feels he has adequately described the night and its resulting blessings.

23. An explanation of the fourth verse. A description of the soul's hiding place.

"In concealment" refers to the security experienced at this time, when one walks in darkness, hidden from the devil. Infused contemplation frees and hides the soul, for it is infused passively without the use of the exterior and interior faculties of the sensory part of a person, and thus free from any obstacles these faculties can cause. Such a person is also free from the influences of the devil who without these faculties of the sensory part cannot reach the inner spirit or know what is happening within it. In this darkness there is more room for spiritual communication without hindrance from the sensory part. While the devil is ignorant of these spiritual communications, he can see that something is happening because of the quietude and silence caused in the sensory part. While the devil cannot affect the spiritual part, he does all he can to disturb the sensory and thus disquiet the spiritual part in its reception of spiritual goods. But, contemplation produces strength in the spirit against these attacks, and leaves the soul with greater peace and security. Of course, if the spiritual communication is given not exclusively to the spirit but to the senses too, then the devil can disturb, torment, and cause considerable pain in the senses. God allows the devil to see some of the favors granted and to disturb, deceive, and challenge the individual where he can, so that when a person is victorious and faithful the rewards are greater. If it should happen that the devil prevails for a while, then the pain is indeed great. This diabolical communication is from spirit to spirit, passively experienced, and violent. If this happens it is so the individual can be further purified. Soon after the torment greater graces are granted directly by God, greater than all previous blessings, bringing delight and peace unhindered by the sensory part. No one attains these blessings without total nakedness and purification in darkness and concealment. At this point a person becomes totally spiritual in the highest degree of prayer and intimacy with God, passions and appetites are eliminated, "my house being now all stilled."

24. Concluding explanation of the second stanza.

Since the superior part of the soul is now, like the lower, at rest in appetites and faculties, a person goes to divine union with God through love, with peace in both sensory and spiritual parts. Through God's influence the individual obtains habitually perfect rest and quietude, is personally touched by the divinity, thus purified, quieted, strengthened, and made stable to receive permanently divine union. When thus united to God in all its members, the individual finds a new bond in the possession of love. One cannot reach this union without remarkable purity which has been attained by vigorous mortification and detachment from all creatures, the radical work of God in the soul.

25. A brief explanation of the third stanza.

Here the individual enumerates and extols the good properties of the night, by which he or she has obtained the desired goal of security. First property, having been led by a solitary and secret contemplation nothing pertaining to senses can any longer detain the soul on this journey to union. Second property, the person is free of all hindrance from forms and figures of natural apprehensions in the faculties that usually prevent him or her from being united with God. Third property, love alone is what guides and moves an individual; one has no support of any particular interior light of intellect and no guide. Deprived of all satisfactions in dense darkness the individual soars to God in an unknown way along the road of solitude, on that glad night.

CHAPTER SIX
FIVE KEY SPIRITUAL CHALLENGES OF THE BOOK OF THE DARK NIGHT

The spiritual challenges of the *Dark Night* are many and profound. Its image of God as at times hidden and at times revealed gives a solid theological foundation for all else. The otherness of God linked to God's personal love for each person reminds us of the sense of transcendence and mystery on the one hand and the immanence and closeness that characterize Christianity. Throughout the entire book, John offers Jesus as a model of love, the incarnation of the love of the Father. John's portrait of the human being, never abstract but always a person in situation in need of transformation, becomes a very challenging understanding of the human vocation to authenticity. John's ascetical teachings and his call for a re-education of the affectivity form one of the most demanding approaches to personal purification that exists in Christian spirituality. Then, John's presentation of the seven deadly sins transposed to a spiritual level, his exciting introduction of the ladder of love, and his unique approach to the theological virtues, are all singularly important contributions to the history of spirituality. John's vision of the night of faith, his original perspective of hope, and the rebirth of love form a wonderful explanation of the core values of our spiritual dedication.

In this chapter we have selected five key spiritual challenges of the book of the *Dark Night*. First, we will study John's teaching on contemplation. Second, we will reflect on his insight of finding one's identity beyond suffering. Third, we will follow John's challenge of always seeing the world through the lens of love. Fourth, we will focus on John's call to be transformed into who we are called to be. Finally, we will seek to pursue with John the constant desire to be enthusiastic about life with God.

Welcoming God in contemplation

The secret of John's system, as it was of his own life, is to always seek God through the nights to renewal and union. While this search affects every aspect of our lives, it is achieved primarily through contemplative prayer and our response to that experience. John sees contemplation in the two parts of the passive nights, and so in some ways the book of the *Dark Night* is a book on contemplation. Contemplation is a call to welcome God into our lives. The first phase of contemplation is the purification and transformation of prayer from discursive meditation to infused prayer beyond rational processes, a development fostered by God within a person who is willing to let go of previous forms of communication with God. This may begin in consolation in prayer but may become a painful process, and John calls it a dark night of purifying contemplation (N.1. Explanation.2) and tells us that it "signifies here purgative contemplation, which passively causes in the soul this negation of self and of all things" (N.1. Explanation.1). A person can make this spiritual journey to contemplation because of the strength and warmth gained from love of Christ in the contemplation (N.1. Explanation.2; 10.6). Gradually God draws a person towards contemplative prayer. "Ordinarily this contemplation . . . imparts to the soul together with the dryness and emptiness it produces in the senses, an inclination to remain alone and in quietude" (N.1. 9.6). So, contemplation purifies, illumines, and nourishes, but John advises that one must not hinder this progress but allow God to work this transformation. Those called to this passive night of contemplation will at first find no satisfaction in meditation or thinking of God, and may think they cannot pray and are not serving God. They become powerless to meditate. All this is because in contemplation God communicates self in a different way, "by an act of simple contemplation" (N.1. 9.8). Those who wish to welcome God into their lives must first welcome this purification of former ways of knowing and loving, they must abandon a spirituality of accumulated ideas and thoughts, and "must be content simply with a loving and peaceful attentiveness to God" (N.1. 10. 3 and 4).

A person shows how much he or she wishes to welcome God into his or her heart primarily by not being a hindrance through activities of the faculties. John told one of his directees, "If you wish to attain holy recollection, you will do so not by receiving but by denying" (S. 52). This can be painful, since it means abandoning what we formerly cherished. However, each one should remain in peace and emptiness, open to the rekindling of love that God's gift of contemplation brings. Contemplation brings a deeper understanding of self and of one's inability to make progress without God's help. As one welcomes God's support, love, and knowledge, a gradual transformation takes place that in time brings humility, peace, and a desire to receive the wisdom and love of God. In addition, this contemplative purification and transformation endow a person with love of neighbor, submissiveness to God, a correction of failings, and a clear direction of life to all that is of God.

The second phase of contemplation is the purification and transformation of one's ways of knowing, remembering, and loving God. John gives a detailed description of the nature, signs, and effects of this night (see N.2. 5). While the first phase transforms our ways of communicating with God in prayer by purifying the use of our senses, it is insufficient (N.2. 2.1). So this second phase transforms what we know of God by purifying our three spiritual faculties of intellect, memory, and will. When John describes this purification he calls it poverty and nakedness, but these two concepts should not be understood statically but rather dynamically—a person is constantly becoming poorer as he or she gives away previously acquired knowledge and is constantly being stripped of all that formerly covered over his or her weak understandings of God (see N.2. 6.1). "Through this contemplation, God teaches the soul secretly and instructs it in the perfection of love without its doing anything or understanding how this happens" (N.2. 5.1). It is a painful experience as God changes our ways of knowing, remembering, and loving God—John calls it "that frightful night of contemplation" (N.2. 1.1), as everything we felt gave value to our spiritual life is now lost (N.2. 6.2 and 5). However, the purification is a preparation for intense love. It lasts in differing amounts of time for different people depending on its intensity (N.2. 8.2). But this contemplation also illumines the intellect, focuses the memory on hope, and enkindles the will in true love. In fact, contemplation is a dark night not because it causes the absence of light but because there is too much light (see N.2. 9.1). As we read in the Liturgy of the Hours, "Tis only the splendor of light hideth thee" (Week 4, Saturday, Readings).

The dark night of contemplation has two rhythms, a conceptual rhythm of knowing/unknowing that purifies our preconceptions of God by eliminating false or inadequate images, teaching us that God is not like any images we may have. The second rhythm is a vital one, a very painful part that takes place in the passive experience of the *Dark Night*, and this teaches us that God does not correspond to our ideas about divine life, nor does God act in the way we expect God to act. Thus, in contemplation God challenges us to abandon our previous knowledge and awareness and dedicate ourselves confidently and peacefully to a divine reality we do not fully understand.

Our approach to contemplation, therefore, includes a series of presuppositions that need to be kept in mind when reading John. John reminds us that there is a relationship between the way we know God and the way we love God; that God reveals self to us in a very personal way. This implies the most fundamental belief that God exists apart from the created world but in love interacts with this world and especially lovingly acts with each of us individually, transforming us to be suitable for life with God. John insists we are made for God and can only find our fulfillment in union with God. This union in love presumes knowledge of God which itself is a gift, since we cannot come to know or love God through our own abilities. This union of knowledge and love is what we call contemplation. Contemplation is prayer and a way of life.

John insists we do not earn contemplation, but God draws us to this new life if God so chooses and if we are prepared and made to have the capacity by God. However, there are a series of qualities, readily found in the life of John of the Cross that can create a suitable environment which could be conducive to a contemplative approach to life. It is important that one has an initial love for Christ and longs to grow into the person he or she is capable of being. Such a person must learn to become comfortable in solitude, meditation, perhaps even isolation, while desiring to become free through love for the will of God in detachment from all that is not movement towards God. It is also valuable that such a one can experience the beautiful wherever it can be appreciated, and be capable of joy and enthusiasm.

Along with these qualities there are other factors that help a person prepare remotely to be a prayerful person whom God may wish to draw to contemplative prayer. One can begin to control and educate one's body, mind, and emotions in all functions by fasting, temperance, and attention to desires, thoughts, attitudes, and feelings. One can choose or create a sacred space which is conducive to recollection and the uplifting of the spirit. Likewise, a person can establish sacred time, making sure opportunities for prayer are adequate and at times open-ended, although not much longer than an hour at a time. Posture is also important; one should choose a position that helps one to be recollected, generally erect and comfortable. Finally, one needs nourishment for the spiritual life; the good food of sound biblical, spiritual, and theological readings. John told a disciples, "Seek in reading and you will find in meditation; knock in prayer and it will be opened to you in contemplation" (S. 158).

Clearly no one can earn the gift of contemplation, but we can prepare ourselves with the daily dedication to stillness of our bodies, to being open and attentive to the inspirations of the Holy Spirit, to concentrate with Christ, and to practice silence in God. We can do all this by fostering an awareness of the presence of God, a spirit of recollection, the cultivation of a sense of wonder, a healthy sense of aloneness, and the patience and willingness to wait. However, when all is said and done contemplation is a gift. It is true that in John there are traces of acquired contemplation—that part of contemplation that includes our active contribution to the gifts of grace. This teaching of John is important and challenging, but it is more of a readying of ourselves for God's interventions and work of prayer in us. Nevertheless, the main effects of contemplation are the passive purification and transformation of our ways of communicating with God and appreciating who God is for us.

In contemplation a person may experience that God is present to him or her. It is an immediate and direct contact with God even though it may not be felt or known. It can also be an experience that includes an intuition which is intense, profound, and very simple. In contemplation a person is moved passively by God. It is more a journey of unknowing rather than knowing (N.2. 17.7). This is an experience which is not in words but in love, and so it is ineffable. It is an infusion of knowledge and love and is given in different ways and degrees to people who are particularly purified of self-centeredness and committed to love and desire for the will of God. Contemplation has great sanctifying qualities.

Contemplation leads to a renewal of life, to a wisdom in our knowledge of God, and to union with God in love. It is an enlightenment, an expansion of consciousness, and a great awakening. It produces forgetfulness of self, a desire to do God's will, a commitment to the service of others. It brings a person inner peace, increased spiritual strength, and personal fulfillment. Contemplation is humanity's greatest opportunity to welcome God into life. This is the light that comes with darkness. This second phase of contemplation is a preparation for union in love (N.2. 9.4), thus John calls it the "loving fire of contemplation" (N.2. 10.2). John complements these ideas on contemplation in the *Dark Night* with insights into union in the *Spiritual Canticle* and the *Living Flame*.

Finding one's identity beyond suffering

John saw his sufferings in prison in Toledo as darkness before the dawn, a glad night that led to transformation in love. As he welcomed his transformative sufferings, John became a different person because of suffering. Not only for him, but for all of us there are important links between suffering and faith. Early Christians chose the crucifix as an image of the essence of Jesus' life and teachings, and when they gathered as a community they did so to remember the Lord's passion ("memoria passionis"). They believed in the redemptive value of suffering when linked to love, and Christians of every age give a special authority to suffering for love. John had no interest in suffering for its own sake. On the contrary, contemporaries affirm that he had a very pleasant personality, enjoyed life and people, loved the outdoors, and delighted in friendships. John also practiced discretion in austerities and criticized those who "burden themselves with extraordinary penances" (A.1. 8.4). However, he pursued love (for him "todo") and was willing to do whatever was necessary to achieve his goal (for him always "nada"). "What profit is there in anything that is not the love of God, and what value has it in God's sight? Love is not perfect if it is not strong and discreet in purifying joy with respect to all things, centering it only on God's will" (A.3. 30.5). So, strong love accepts negation and suffering; this is a fundamental pillar of John's vision of life. "One cannot reach this union without remarkable purity, and this purity is unattainable without vigorous mortification and nakedness regarding all creatures" (N.2. 24.4).

The acceptance of suffering—for John negation, purification, emptiness, and nakedness—takes place in two phases. The first is the result of one's active involvement in the purification of his or her appetites or false attachments—this is the work of the active nights, and we find John's many recommendations for this phase on his diagram of Mount Carmel, and in his detailed description in the *Ascent*. "If a soul has more patience in suffering and more forebearance in going without satisfaction, the sign is there of its being more proficient in virtue" (S. 120). Part of this involvement is confronting the consequences suffering has on others wherever we find them. Included in this active purification would be one's efforts to combat and alleviate sickness, loss of dignity and love, problems in employment, consequences of natural disasters, evils of war, injustices, marginalization, and all forms of violence. "See that you are not suddenly saddened by the adversities of this world, for you do not know the good they bring, being ordained in the judgments of God for the everlasting joy of the elect" (S. 64). When suffering is the result not of love but of hatred, then each one must confront it, remove it, never forget it, and respond to it in love and service.

The second phase is the result of the acceptance of the pain that inflicts a person in the passive nights—a pain at times so strong one cannot explain it (A Prologue.1). "God proceeds thus so that by both withdrawing the appetites from other objects and recollecting them in himself, he strengthens the soul and gives it the capacity for this strong union of love, which he begins to accord by means of this purgation" (N.2. 11.3). Suffering's value comes from "this strong union of love," and John's focus is always on the pursuit of the latter. Suffering purifies and prepares one "to receive the strength of this union of love" (N.2 11.3).

John gives the impression that if a person is not pursuing love then he or she is involved in something that is part of the sufferings of this world. All things "compared to all the delight that is God are intense suffering, torment, and bitterness" (A.1. 4.7). So, some suffering is due to the longings of the heart—"impatient love" (F. 3.18)—for a union not yet achieved (C. 6.2). Some suffering is God's gift to those who long for union. "God ordains our sufferings that we may love what we most desire, make greater sacrifices, and be worth more" (L. 11). All this is in imitation of Jesus and his death on the cross for love of humanity. "Crucified inwardly and outwardly with Christ, you will live in this life with fullness and satisfaction of soul, and possess your soul in patience" (S. 87). Each of us is called to accept suffering in imitation of Jesus (L. 25, see also II A 7, 6-7) and for love of God (A.2. 26.10); "suffering for love of him whatever is for his service" (C. 2.5). "In tribulation, immediately draw near to God with trust, and you will receive strength, enlightenment, and instruction" (S. 66). In fact, our desire for knowledge and love of God "is commensurate with suffering for Him" (C. 12.9). Describing the fourth step on the ladder of love, John says, "a habitual yet unwearisome suffering is engendered on account of the Beloved. . . . the soul at this stage through so genuine a love pursues God in the spirit of suffering for his sake" (N.2. 19.4). Again, suffering is for love, and when motivated by love "you will not notice whether you suffer or not" (L. 17).

Suffering on the way to union of love comes from a variety of sources, all part of God's gifts to prepare one for union. The illumination of contemplation brings with it the pain that comes from seeing one's own defects. As a person loses former prayer forms and religious satisfaction, he or she feels the pain of dryness and emptiness. When a person becomes unable to think of God, he or she can become embittered at the loss of past good things. When all this is taken together, a person suffers from a complete loss of former security as his or her life seems no longer on firm ground. All these sufferings are part of God's strategy of love. "God desires to withdraw them from this base manner of loving and lead them on to a higher degree of divine love" (N.1. 8.3). Besides the suffering that comes from dryness and aridity, there is also the painful experience of the absence of God. "The suffering and pain arising from God's absence is usually so intense in those who are nearing the state of perfection. . . " (C. 1.22; see 2.5).

Suffering is a byproduct of the purification needed for union in love. "Those who have more considerable capacity and strength for suffering, God purges more intensely and quickly" (N.1. 14.5). "[T]here is nothing in contemplation or the divine inflow which of itself can give pain" (N.2. 9.11); rather, the suffering results from one's own weaknesses and imperfections of love (N.2. 10.4). "These imperfections are the fuel that catches on fire, and once they are gone there is nothing left to burn. So, . . . when the imperfections are gone, the soul's suffering terminates, and joy remains" (N.2. 10.5).

So, a person finds his or her own identity beyond suffering and only because of suffering. One's authentic calling can be appreciated only in suffering which becomes the beginning of a newness of life. We must trust suffering in God and realize that we can thus find the life we long for even without looking for it.

Seeing the world through the lens of love

It is common to consider that John presents his readers with the journey of faith in the *Ascent* and the *Dark Night*, and the journey of love in the *Spiritual Canticle* and the *Living Flame of Love*. However, the purpose of the *Dark Night* is to describe a person's conduct "along the spiritual road that leads to the perfect union with God through love" (N. Title). Of course, one only undertakes this journey when one is "fired with love's urgent longings," and one travels "with no other light or guide than the one that burned in my heart," and at the end of the journey, it is "love alone," that makes one soar to God (N.2. 25.4). Perhaps we could describe the *Dark Night* as the journey of strong love (N.2. 11.3; see C. 31.4). From start to end John's approach is "nor have I any other work now that my every act is love" (C. v. 28), and overriding every other conviction is "When evening comes you will be examined in love" (S. 60).

The major transformation of love takes place in the passive nights when with God's help a person departs "from love of both self and all things. . . so as to reach the sweet and delightful life of love of God" (N.1. Explanation.1). But in this process it is God who draws the person, leads him or her forward, liberates and prepares the soul for the life of love (N.1. 8.3). God achieves this in contemplation, which is "nothing else than a secret and peaceful inflow of God, which, if not hampered, fires the soul in the spirit of love" (N.1. 10.6). By means of this transformation, God empowers a person to see the whole world through the lens of love. This vision of love enthuses John to say, "O sweetest love of God, so little known, whoever has found this rich mine is at rest" (S. 16).

John is always concerned that human love can be divided into thousands of affections and desires. What he wants is complete unity of love, totally directed to God. "You shall love the Lord your God with all your heart, and with all your soul, and with all your strength, and with all your mind; and your neighbor as yourself" (Matt 10: 27). The serious tests of the dark nights lead to a unification of all the powers of a person in the union of love. John describes this asceticism of love as a ladder that has ten steps. These are the ten steps of the "science of love," "an infused loving knowledge that both illumines and enamors the soul, elevating it step by step to God, its Creator. For it is only love that unites and joins the soul to God" (N.2. 18.5).

The first step on the ladder of love is when God gifts a person with the sense of dissatisfaction and sickness with the way things are going in life. This languishing is partly due to an awareness of one's own failings, but it also includes a yearning for a changed life. The second step develops from the first and consists in a person's relentless pursuit of God. This is the result of God's gift of love, and the soul now seeks only God in every aspect of life. Moreover, this is also a time when one leaves aside any image of God of his or her own creation and searches in love for the true God. The third step is when a person performs good works as part of his or her total self-gift to God. He or she works without ceasing for fear a response might be inadequate. A person on this step of the ladder becomes more aware of his or her failings and yet wants to act unceasingly for the love of God. The fourth step is an important development of love, for a person now pursues God without fail in spite of any sufferings that may come in the way. Giving himself or herself to pleasing God at all costs, the soul is now committed to self-control and is now ready to pay the cost of love. Step five on the ladder of love is when a person receives from God an impatient desire and an ardent longing for God. All one's strength is now focused on the pursuit of God, and he or she becomes impatient, as the yearning at times seems frustrated.

All these steps on the ladder are the result of God's gifts of love that draw a person to higher steps. The fifth step leads into the sixth when a person's hope invigorates him or her to further purification and love in the pursuit of God. John describes the seventh step as an ardent boldness when a person centers his or her life totally on God's love. The individual is no longer satisfied with a moderate response to God and does not want to hold back development in any way, but receives courage to respond with boldness. Thus, God gives the soul a participation in the strength and daring of divine love. The eighth step happens when an individual is united to God in love even though not continually. In this intermittent, actual union, each one now senses that he or she can reach out for God or be drawn to God by the infusion of love. The ninth step is when the Holy Spirit causes the person to sense the presence of God's love in his or her life. It is a time of satisfaction in the blessings of God, and the soul feels this is what he or she has been longing for—habitual union. The final step is the union of an individual with God in afterlife, as he or she is totally purified and transformed by God's love.

In the *Spiritual Canticle* John stated his understanding very clearly. "It is noteworthy that any soul with authentic love cannot be satisfied until it really possesses God. Everything else not only fails to satisfy it but . . . increases the hunger and appetite to see him as he is" (C. 6.4). After the purification and enkindling of love John can affirm, "O Great God of love, and Lord! How many riches do you place in the soul that neither loves nor is satisfied save in you alone, for you give yourself to it and become one with it through love" (L. 11). This love transforms a person (S. 29) and fills him or her with love of neighbor too.

In our contemporary world where a continued lack of love threatens to burst frozen hearts, John's vision of a world dedicated to love is revolutionary. It is important to remember that the intensities of the journey through the dark nights do not turn people in on themselves in a focus of selfish personal development, but rather opens them to the loving service of others. More than anything else, the book of the *Dark Night* deals with how God works to draw a person to divine life; this is God's strategy of selfless love that becomes a model for our approach to the whole of life. God teaches us how to love (see N.2. 5.1), purifies selfishness so that a person can love one's neighbor (see N.1. 12.8), and calls us to show forgiveness (S. 47). John has a guiding principle for all we do; "Where there is no love, put love, and you will draw out love" (L. 26). At the end of the nights love is strong, one is transformed, one is trained to be recollected, and an individual is sensitive to the Spirit and in union with the will of God, and one's contemplation arouses a longing for the complete union of love. Love is the gift, the motivation, the goal, and the reward of this journey. "The ultimate reason for everything is love" (C. 38.5).

Being transformed into who we are called to be

In his own journey of faith and love, John was ever dedicated to the two-fold goal of union with God and total renewal of self. One of his most distinctive characteristics was his readiness to deny himself anything for love and for the desire to reach his goal. He knew that "The soul who does not know how to lose herself does not find herself" (C. 29.11). For John, personal transformation was a byproduct of the search for union with God. However, for those with lesser motivation he could still insist that giving oneself to the pursuit of the love of God has some very nice secondary results. "Even if human beings do not free their hearts of joy in temporal goods for the sake of God and the demands of Christian perfection, they ought to do so because of the resulting temporal advantages, prescinding from the spiritual ones. . . . [They] acquire the virtue of liberality. . . . Moreover, they acquire liberty of spirit, clarity of reason, rest, tranquility, peaceful confidence in God. . . . They obtain more joy and recreation in creatures. . . . In detachment from things they acquire a clearer knowledge of them" (A.3. 20.2). John experienced the benefits of this transformation, as we see in the beauty of his poetry, his perceptiveness in spiritual direction, his warmth and affection in dealing with others, his empathy for his directees, and the peace and resignation of his last months.

The primary purpose of human development is to prepare oneself for union with God, and we can never be satisfied unless and until we are filled with divine life in loving union (see F. 1.12). The poverty and nakedness of the nights do not leave us empty but rather lead to real joy in the Spirit and satisfaction in life. "Oh, what a sheer grace it is for the soul to be freed from the house of its senses. . . . [Such people] will understand how the life of the spirit is true freedom and wealth and embodies inestimable goods" (N.2. 14.3). This renewal includes the spiritual, religious, and sense levels of life. So, even the senses are all exercised with a new force and under the guidance of the spirit. It is clear from John's diagram of Mount Carmel that he saw the goal of the journey through the nights as the immersion in the gifts of the Holy Spirit which he places all around the peak of Mount Carmel. The goal includes the profound enrichment of life. The journey through the nights does not drain us of our humanity but refines and redirects the best qualities of which human beings are capable; it is a journey to human fulfillment.

One of the most important components of a person's transformation into what he or she is called to be is God's impact on life by means of the three theological virtues. By redirecting intellect, memory, and will to their God-directed objects of faith, hope, and love, God enables a person to reach his or her full potential (see N.2. 4.2). The intellect should not get bogged down in objects of knowledge or information especially about God, but rather should focus on the knowledge of God which is faith. The memory wastes its energy and consciousness for the present thinking of past gifts or diminishments and the feelings and influences attached to them when the real object of a person's yearnings should be the hope of union with God. The will can disperse its energy so easily on multiple objects of desire, but reaches its God-given power when totally integrated in one unified act of love of all that is of God. These three powers of the human spirit are what make us who we are. The Fathers of the Church even defined a human being as "capax Dei;" the only creature capable of knowing, longing for, and loving God. However, in the *Dark Night* John is not referring to moral virtues—what individuals can do, but emphasizing the passive manner in which these theological virtues are experienced. It is as if he identifies them with what happens in contemplation. John speaks of these three virtues as a disguise which the soul wears to make itself more pleasing to God and to enable it to hide from, and thereby overcome, the great evils of the world (see N.2. 21).

While faith includes the teachings of the Church and the ecclesial community's self-understanding, it is particularly faith as the experience of God that John emphasizes. "Faith . . . gives and communicates God himself to us" (C. 12.4; see C. 1.10). John's approach to faith is very concrete—in his views of the Church and its teachings, and also mystical—in his emphasis on the ineffable experience. "And just as God is darkness to our intellect, so faith dazzles and blinds us. Only by means of faith, in divine light exceeding all understanding, does God manifest himself to the soul. The greater one's faith the closer is one's union with God" (A.2. 9.1).

Hope is the most fundamental attitude of people of faith. We have faith in what we hope for, and without hope our faith can become empty words. What we hope for is the fullness of the life we experience in faith. John so wants us to keep our gaze fixed on the vision of hope in God that he enlikens hope to a helmet, but describes it almost as blinders that stop us looking from side to side and keep us focused on the hope ahead (N.2. 21.7). Through God's transformation in contemplative prayer a person lives in forgetfulness (see A.3. 9.4) of the objects of memory (see A.3. 11) and instead strives for "union of the memory with God through perfect hope" (N.2. 11.2). God moves a person to deepen hope and leave memories aside; to strive for "hope in God alone," and without this hope nothing is gained, "since what moves and conquers is unrelenting hope" (N.2. 21.8). Our memories help us hold on or possess the past and anticipate what may not really be the future. What John wants us to do is to strive to possess God, and we do that by receiving God's gift of hope (see N.2. 21.9).

The third component of God's transforming gift is true love. "Charity also empties and annihilates the affections and appetites of the will of whatever is not God and centers them on Him alone. Thus charity prepares the will and unites it with God through love" (N.2. 21.11). Charity is "the finishing touch," and it "adds elegance to the other two," and "elevates the soul as to place her near God." Moreover, "where there is true love of God, love of self and of one's own things finds no entry," and "without charity no virtue is pleasing to God" (N.2. 21.10).

So, this transforming gift of God's love is what this journey has been about—a striving for knowledge of and hope in God permeated with love. Contemplation, the science of love, "is an infused loving knowledge that both illumines and enamors the soul, elevating it step by step to God, its Creator. For it is only love that unites and joins the soul to God" (N.2. 18.5). This is a journey in which we come to realize that God has already always been with us and one in which God draws us to divine life in deepening love, drawing us towards union in love. It is more foundationally about God's love for us rather than our love for God—we simply accept God's transforming love in our lives (see S. 90).

These three great energies that God places within us enable us to become who we are capable of being, reaching our full potential in lives given to God. "Because these virtues have the function of withdrawing the soul from all that is less than God, they consequently have the mission of joining it with God" (N.2. 21.11). When so many contemporary lives, even those of religious people, are absorbed in trivial ideas, hopes, and loves, John challenges us to be who we are capable of being, to let our lives be filled with the greatest thoughts, hopes, and loves that human beings can attain. These are all given to us by God, and as a result of these gifts all aspects of our lives can be integrated, transforming us and our world.

Being enthusiastic about life with God

We are people transformed by faith, and the most immediate consequence of faith is our conviction that there is more in life than meets the eye; there is a world that is not immediately apparent. Our experience of faith teaches us that there are two horizons to life, and they are intimately linked. We discover in ourselves a zone that naturally yearns for transcendent reality, and we live at this level of mystery, where we are enthralled by enduring truths. Everything we think and do is transformed by this awareness of a relationship between our everyday life and a realm of life that gives meaning to this one. "I no longer live within myself and I cannot live without God, for having neither him nor myself what will life be? It will be a thousand deaths, longing for my true life and dying because I do not die" (Stanzas of the soul that suffers with longing to see God, v. 1). Again, here, life is judged and given a new meaning by a horizon of life beyond this one.

Through the dark nights we are longing to find our true lives, and John teaches us that as people of faith we should naturally identify with the transcendent. John gives the impression of being someone totally dedicated to all that he is doing here in this world while at the same time being elsewhere, enjoying life on another horizon. This requires a spirit of reflection and a hunger for silence. When we emerge from tranformative silence we have an ability to view the world through a different lens that can change everything for us. Deep within each of us there is a yearning for union with God. John insists that this process of discovering the potential for growth that lies within us includes distancing ourselves from the accumulation of religious devotions and entering with simplicity into our own hearts. We seek the richness of life not by adding on more religious practices but by touching ultimate goodness and love that lie within us. Appreciating God's gift of love (see "Romances") and encountering the everlasting call of God in our own hearts, we then see that our faith experience guides the course of life. We need to pay attention to the connections between our own yearnings for fulfillment and the call of another realm of life. As we journey through life we catch a glimpse of a horizon of life beyond this one. This is one of the foundational experiences of our spirituality. The world in which we live only has meaning because of a realm of life of which we catch sight from time to time. We are not journeying in the unknown, even when we journey through the dark nights, for we can still feel a certain companionship of our God who draws us to divine life (N.2. 11.7).

John is excited and enthusiastic about this journey through the dark nights, "Ah! The sheer grace!" The journey through the dark nights is a "departure from the fetters and straits of the senses" (N.1. 11.3) and so it is a joyful liberation. Again the passive night of spirit brings joy and peace. "It was a sheer grace for this soul that God in this night puts to sleep. . . all the faculties, passions, affections, and appetites that live in its sensory and spiritual parts" (N.2. 14.2). In the resulting emptiness a person finds peace, freed from possessions that can take possession of a person. During the journey to God an individual is moved by solicitude for God's love (see N.1. 11.2). Having endured the passive night of sense, "The soul readily finds in its spirit, without the work of meditation, a very serene, loving contemplation and spiritual delight" (N.2. 1.1). Even during the passive night of spirit there are times of respite and joy. "Then the soul, like one who has been unshackled and released from a dungeon and who can enjoy the benefit of spaciousness and freedom, experiences great sweetness of peace and loving friendship with God in a ready abundance of spiritual communication" (N.2. 7.4). Still the soul feels something is lacking and yearns for more. At the end of the journey to God we find "that sublime and joyous union with God" (N. Prologue). So, joy and peace and further longings punctuate this journey through the nights, undertaken as it is with enthusiasm.

One of the great fruits of the passive night of spirit which enthuses John is a vehement passion of divine love. A person longs for God with the desire and anxiety of love. This enthusiastic love is God's gift, an initial capacity for union in love (see N.2. 11). It is an urgent longing, an inebriation, a strength, a vehemence, a bold energy; everything seems possible, the only important thing is to pursue deeper love of God (see N.2. 13.7-8). Moreover, in this dark night of the spirit a person finds security, protected from all that is not God (see N.2. 16). He or she realizes that this call of God is a secret wisdom, a mystical theology that catches him or her up in the love of God and in an awareness of the baseness of all else in comparison with God (see N.2. 17). This experience is above all a ladder of love that individuals enthusiastically climb to even stronger love (N.2. 18-20).

It is interesting to read the Letters, *Sayings*, and dedications of the principal works. John is surrounded by a community of faith that is filled with enthusiasm. There is no sense of fear even before the anticipated pain of the nights. Rather, there is peaceful, confident enthusiasm. "Going everywhere, my God, with you, everywhere things will happen as I desire for you" (S. 53). Of course, John has already finished the journey and is looking back, appreciating the transformation God wrought in him. He knows that by God's gifts "the soul is purified, quieted, strengthened, and made stable so she may receive permanently this divine union, which is the divine espousal between the soul and the Son of God" (N.2. 24.3). In this spiritual marriage, "Divine Wisdom is united with the soul in a new bond of the possession of love" (N.2. 24.3). This is the horizon of life that gives meaning to our life in this world. We can all say with the psalmist, "As a deer longs for flowing streams, so my soul longs for you, O God. My soul thirsts for God, for the living God. When shall I come and behold the face of God?" (Ps 42:1-2). John always insisted we must make this journey with enthusiasm, "fired with love's urgent longings."

The entire system of John centers on God, the principal agent in the spiritual life. God draws people to divine life, taking the initiative in every stage of the journey. God's love precedes all human response; it is a love that calls, purifies, illumines, supports in pain, shares, transforms, and unites. "O Lord, my God, who will seek you with simple and pure love, and not find that you are all one can desire, for you show yourself first and go out to meet those who seek you" (S. 2). This journey is thrilling, it is exciting, and we can enter it with enthusiasm.

CHAPTER SEVEN
THE DARK NIGHT IN
CONTEMPORARY LIFE

What is a dark night today?

A dark night is what happens to a dedicated person in his or her journey to God; a journey in which he or she longs to get to know God more accurately and as a result learn to love God more authentically. John's great interest is to help us journey to God in love and in doing so how to deal with all the ups and downs we might encounter on that journey. The dark night is not the end but the means to live in faith, hope, and love and thus move to union with God. When one sets out on a difficult journey, especially the climbing of a mountain, it is so calming to have a good guide who has already made the trip and knows the difficulties one might encounter. If the guide has any common sense, he or she will not describe the journey by enumerating all the difficulties, but by enthusing their fellow travelers with what it is like to get to the goal of the trip. John does precisely that. However, a good guide will never take clients on a trip or a hike that is too difficult for them; they need to be able to confront the hardships and not easily give up or want to go back. In fact, they need to be trained well. There are always some guides who will want to take their followers on easy trips that readily please but are not too challenging. I have hiked a lot in the United States National Parks and thoroughly enjoyed the pleasant experiences, and I will no doubt do it again; most trails are not very difficult or demanding. I have also climbed in the Alps, ended up exhausted, totally worn out, and unable even to move from fatigue, but these climbs are among the most exciting and exhilarating experiences of my life. When you struggle to the top of a mountain and look both up and down you not only have a different view of the mountain, but you also have a different view of yourself and of your world. However, such climbs are difficult and demanding and need a lot of training.

John has already climbed Mount Carmel, he knows the way well, and has more than once—both personally and in spiritual direction—seen the obstacles one can encounter and how best to deal with them. John tells us that there are two main problems we will encounter on our journey; at first they may seem only obstacles but actually they are difficult short cuts, and they can energize us to make the journey with greater vigor and enthusiasm. He describes these two great periods of transformation as "nights" of sense and spirit, because at first they seem to confuse and darken the way we have always viewed things, but later they will become experiences of profound illumination. John is a careful guide modeling his way on God's guidance of chosen ones. "And I will lead the blind in a way they know not, in paths that they have not known I will guide them. I will turn the darkness before them into light, the rough places into level ground. These are the things I will do, and I will not forsake them" (Ps 42,16). In the nights of this journey to God we find out how to see things in a different way and how to look at God, self, and life in a different way. We can then echo the words a poet puts into the mouth of God, "Night is my most beautiful creation."[11]

So, John sees this journey to God has having two momentous challenges, a night experience for our senses and a night experience for our spirit. Each of these nights has both an active phase in which we do the work, and a passive phase in which God does the transforming work within us. The night of sense refers to objects or experiences of sense that can lead us to God but can also be obstacles to God. Examples could include objects and places of religious devotions, buildings, places, pilgrimages, books, religious practices, religious people, favorite prayers, devotions to saints, spiritual directors, media personalities, and so on. The problem with all these sense objects of religion is that while they are good in themselves and often helpful, people can become attached to objects that are meant to help move us to God and lose sight of the real goal of getting closer to God. The night of spirit refers to those normal objects of the spiritual faculties of intellect, memory, and will that can lead us to God but can also be obstacles to this encounter. Examples could include hopes, experiences, retreats, commitments in ministry, motivations, understandings of vocation, enthusiasm in projects, delight in spiritual renewal, and more. All these objects of sense or spirit can be wonderful aids in our journey, but we can absolutize them, become attached to them, claim we are principled in clinging to them, and so on. All this presents images that relate to God, images of our own creation. The spiritual journey, more than anything else, is the purifying of images of God, others, ourselves, our roles in life, our vision and mission and purpose in life—all images that impact who God is for us. In the nights we are urged to see all this in a new way, and then to always look at all of this in a new way, until we are left with no further desire for the old ways of relating to God.

Dark nights are crises but not all crises are dark nights. The purification is of sin and sinful tendencies, but much purification of sin precedes the journey, since John says those who make this journey are already resolutely committed to God. The purification of the nights is a purification of appetites—inordinate attachments to something that we thought led us to God. Many of these inordinate desires are now social sins, institutionalized sins, positions that some people often rationalize and support. So, the two dark nights that at first hinder and then re-direct us on our journey to God are at first confusing as we lose the security we formerly had. Then they become illuminating as we see a new way of viewing life and the world. Of course the joy of coming into the light is never so great as when we have been in darkness. Above all, when undergoing this journey we remember that God is guiding us, and with the psalmist we can affirm, "Let only darkness cover me, and the light about me be night, even the darkness is not dark to thee, the night is bright as the day; for darkness is as light with thee" (Ps 139: 11-12).

Some forms of the dark night in contemporary life

Realizing the deity we believed in does not exist.

A contemporary experience of the dark night is "the struggle to maintain faith in a loving God in face of overwhelming evil and suffering in the world and within oneself."[12] John was immersed in the struggles of his own day and witnessed conflict and suffering, becoming as many do today "an unwitting pawn" in other people's conflicts. This led to his imprisonment and his own confrontation with the question of why God would treat him in this way. In his own struggles and pain John gains deeper knowledge of himself and of the transcendence of God. As people today confront their own struggles with mistreatment, abandonment, hatred, torture, and organizational evils, they too "struggle to believe and trust in an all-knowing, all-powerful, all-just, and all-merciful God after a shattering confrontation with the depths of evil in the world and in themselves."[13] How can good people do the things they do? Why is there so much suffering imposed on so many—on a greater scale than ever before? Why is suffering deliberately inflicted as a tool of military and governmental policy? Of course, as Christians and Roman Catholics we have to face the memory of Auschwitz and its horrors, orchestrated and overseen largely by Christians. We see how degraded we can become. This "dangerous memory" is powerful, for when we reflect on it we know we are sinners and that we must change. How can the God we have believed in allow all this? No one can suggest that we come out of this experience or awareness of evil purified and a better, more loving people. We do not! In fact, we often get worse. Instead of the passive nights presenting us with our own personal sinfulness, do they now undermine our former faith by forcing us to confront the horrors of our evil world and totally challenge many aspects of our belief in God? In face of evil do we feel we cannot believe anymore or is it that the God we believed in does not exist anymore? Perhaps this is not a loss of faith but a purification of faith and understandings of God as John expected in the dark night; that we are discovering that God is "far more mysterious than we ever imagined."[14]

Part of these evils is the unchecked reality of on-going, unresolved injustice. We live entrenched in social sin that few people do anything about. It continues in our world and in our churches from one generation to the next, as if we are completely impotent to resolve it. Social injustice is at its roots an unwillingness and an inability to accept the image of a loving God who seeks through men and women to transform our selfish world. Some good people merely work at the margins, leaving the world unchanged and as corrupt and greedy as ever. Social injustice is a dark night in which we cry out for purification and illumination, try to stop discursive explanations and justifications, and we discover who God wants to be for us.

People today may well avoid the introspective analysis of their own sinfulness that could help them focus on the transcendence of God. Perhaps, their helplessness before the evil of our world, humanity's evil, is God's way of showing us how evil we are, how we just don't get it, how helpless we are, how much we need forgiveness, and how much we need God. Then too, as we question God regarding this evil world, we face the reality that God is not the God we thought, nor does God act towards us in the way we expected. The dark night of confrontation of evil is a passive night, we suffer immersed in it, finding much of what we previously valued is now lost. We are helpless, unable to understand ourselves or the God in whom we formerly believed. Perhaps it can be a transforming night when we encounter God, different than we expected, calling us to be different than we have ever been.

The Church's long dark winter's night.

In the experience of the dark night there comes a point when everything we formerly valued seems to be falling apart. At this time, we simply do not know what to do; we feel lost and without a sense of direction, nor does God intervene to help us out. In fact, it seems God has abandoned us or even rejected everything about us. This is not only a description of our own personal journey, but a more than adequate description of the struggles many have in the Church today. The ongoing crisis of the Christian Churches is "a long dark winter's night"[15] that calls out for a passive night of purification.

Many readers undoubtedly grew up very comfortable in their Church and possibly responded with enthusiasm to the challenges of renewal of the Second Vatican Council. But now many feel strangers in the Church, and find its teachings no longer seem meaningful to them as before, and faith as right thinking no longer the support of daily life as it used to be. Some Christians, today, stress that they are "conservative" Catholics or "liberal" Catholics, thus emphasizing a particular image they have, an appetite, to approach the Church with a particular psychological or sociological focus. Many dedicated people we know find that today they are outsiders to the Church they have loved so much, they no longer "practice" by weekly attendance, and they feel that the Church is not as relevant to modern life as they once found it to be. So, many see themselves as Christian and more deeply spiritual than ever, but having formerly found their identity in the Church, they now experience darkness.

These same people would love to have leaders they could admire and trust, men and women of profound spiritual commitment. They long for a sense of ecclesial vision, experience of community, and spiritual leadership. Unfortunately, they are overwhelmed with problems. All over the world the Church faces sexual scandals, bankruptcies, church closings and fights with parishioners, financial mismanagement, silencing of theologians, and much more. Unfortunately, these are the issues that non-Christians see discussed about the Church, and even the faithful feel a profound loss of confidence.

In the dark night our image of God dies, and God then gives us a new image of divine life. Likewise, with profound sadness we see that for many believers the former image of the Church is dying, and many in the Church are attached to sense objects and appetites that need purification as a first step to renewal. It is easy to say the Church is always wonderful and always sinful, but for many nothing seems to change. Rather, they see a helpless clinging to old ways that needs a passive purgation of a dark night for leaders and followers alike, so that the Church can once again satisfy the yearnings of the human heart. For people who have loved the Church and now feel sad, abandoned, and hopeless, the application of the ladder of love to the Church could lead this long winter's night into a transforming dawn.

Vocations in troubled times.

All people who love the Church are saddened by the problems facing specific vocational dedication in the Church, whether priesthood, religious life, or married life. Not only must we face problems of declining numbers, clear differences in interpretation of roles and calling, but also sexual misconduct, all kinds of abuse, and financial scandals that have rocked the Church. Times like these have happened in the Church in previous centuries, but never to this extent in our own generation. While some may think it appropriate to relate these problems to the old church of Europe or the United States, it is equally clear that some of the younger churches have severe problems, some of them evident and others below the surface but well-known. We must sadly acknowledge that many communities are becoming exclusively retirement communities, filled with elderly religious. Some priests and religious must work into their later years to financially support their communities and maintain some appearance of responding to the pastoral needs they formerly covered with ease. Communities are dying, seminaries are empty, and some religious and priests still leave. These crises touch the heart of consecration, the quality of spiritual life, and the hopes and yearnings of a Church that wishes to be faithful to its calling.

To suggest all this is the result of secularization, consumer society, the fault of modernism, and increasing egoism is very superficial, for we live in a time of increased dedication and a yearning for spirituality. Is it that there is something wrong with the contemporary image of priesthood and religious life? Have they both lost their appeal, not because of decreased dedication of the young, but because these vocations in their present form in contemporary life do not seem as relevant as they used to be. In both cases some outstanding issues such as religious habit, forms of poverty, religious practices, community structures, clerical celibacy, forms of power and authority, gender issues, are all sense objects that need both active and passive purification. In other cases forms of consecration, interpretation of vows, structures of religious devotions, impact of central Vatican control, contemporary significance of charisms, ministry agendas, and community mission need passive purification of spirit.

All the goodness that brought us to where we are will not get us where we need to be. We are in a profound darkness, and we cannot get out of it on our own. Psychological, sociological, religious, and spiritual analyses (active night responses) will help, but in the end we need to face our own helplessness, sinfulness, and inability to resolve these issues on our own. We must be purified by God as Church in the passive nights and open our hearts to discover not what we want the future to be but what God wants the future to be. There comes a time when it is desirable to let certain structures and forms of dedication die so that God can bring forth new ones that we cannot even imagine. In the dark night images die and a new reality emerges as a gift from God. If we do not accept the darkness, we can never appreciate that this darkness can be a guiding light. If we deliberately prolong the darkness, we prevent the Church from ever being purified by the brightness of God's renewed love for a changing Church.[16]

Married couples face "Dark Nights and Hard Days"

Married couples also face difficult times in their life together, "Dark Nights and Hard Days" in the development of their own vocation. Even the most dedicated and romantic couple must face the darkness of their spiritual journey. "The couple's task of dealing with changing values, significant life events, adult development stages, family life transitions, rites of passage, shifts from codependency to autonomy, and a host of other normal life experiences plunges the couple into a darkness filled with hard questions."[17] This is a time of refocusing on a new vision of life together, letting go of the old approaches they cherished, and opening to an unknown God-given future. The first, early stage of marriage is gratifying in its love, and both find it profoundly satisfying, but this is an immature phase.[18] Nevertheless, couples like to cling to this phase, and if they do they block development and future enrichment. Then, secondly, as one of the couple yearns to be different conflicts arise. "Both partners enter into a period of darkness, but for the person who has been surprised by this shift, the darkness is amplified by feelings of emptiness, betrayal, hurt, and anger."[19] It is painful to leave behind what they cherished, but it is no longer enough. The third stage becomes one of purification as the couple sees their own failings in contrast to their ideal. "The couple needs extraordinary strength as they experience this stage of development, since they are being asked, through the call of a more authentic love, to let go of their images of one another and meet honestly face-to-face for the first time."[20] The fourth stage is one of uncertainty as the couple moves to personal equality. This intense period is also one of discovery that the other is not who one thought he or she to be. This leads in a fifth stage to a time of relentless conflict, darkness, and emptiness, when nothing seems to work and each one feels helpless. Stage six is a movement back to the union of mature love with a new sense of surrender and a deeper mutual spirituality. The final stage is dawn after darkness, a transformation under God, a more mature mutuality, a deeper intimacy and love.

John in describing the journey of love speaks about union, union in absence, absence in union, and full union. There are clear parallels to the purification of sense and spirit in these stages. The couple in early life together wants to stay as they are, savoring the satisfaction they share. Gradually they are drawn out of this comfort by events beyond their control and find themselves in pain, emptiness, and abandonment. It is a purifying experience as they miss past good things and have no idea what lies ahead. If they are faithful in this darkness and trust their love to God, God draws them through these trials and into a deeper union. After all, the "dark night" is a love poem. Their dark night becomes a guiding night, a night more lovely than the dawn, a night that unites the lover with the beloved, transforming the beloved in her lover (N. v. 5). So, "the way of spiritual negation is by no means a denial of the erotic, sensual, romantic dimensions of human life; rather it gathers them up and carries them to profound new levels."[21] Clearly, not all crises in marriage are dark nights in John's sense, but some are. When all aspects of married life including conjugal spirituality are integrated in total unified gift to God, then this journey, too, becomes a profound spiritual purification, a re-awakening, and a discovery of new love.

Darkness over the earth.

In some contemporary situations such as those mentioned above, there are clear parallels between John's teachings on the dark night and these experiences. It is possible to apply the metaphor of the night and its spiritual challenges to such cases as those mentioned. We also find people referring to the dark nights of illness, depression, addiction, and so on. Sometimes there are common traits, but often it is not appropriate to see basic human crises and trials as being equal to the profound spiritual experience to which John refers, even though at times they can help precipitate a dark night. Nevertheless, there is no problem in using John's advice to help in whatever crises we face. John shows how we can grow through crises, and we can respond to any crisis with similar confidence, following his advice.

Often there are crises which are not dark nights in John's classical sense, but these same crises can provoke dark night experiences in spiritually sensitive observers or participants. Thus, our political and social fabric is going through crises of unprecedented proportions. In recent years we have seen several political leaders gain power and then quickly become dictators, depriving their people of basic rights. Others, once in power, totally ignore the rightful democratic aspirations of the people, seeing democracy merely as the ballot box after which those elected can do what they like. We have governments in developed nations that are completely broken, led largely by old men attached to their positions, bereft of any new ideas, simply prolonging the status quo that gives them status, power, and wealth. In recent years we have witnessed large sections of the financial and business communities destroyed by their own greed, lack of ethics, and insatiable desire to feed off other people's artificially created misfortune. We have seen healthcare industry providers become parasites, bringing sickness instead of health, death instead of cures, as they prostitute their values without offering us hope of relief.

When we examine the common situations of our politicians, financial, business, and healthcare leaders, we see much selfishness, greed, hunger for power, and a disdain for ordinary members of the community. There are many good people it is true, but at times the evils of these organizations overwhelm any trace of goodness. To all this we can add the destruction of our environment by those who have no interest in the future and seek only short term gain. Even our environment is crying in its pain. Many of these dysfunctional individuals are completely incapable of changing, bogged down in a sinfulness that now seems endemic to structures originally formed to aid the community. Obviously, these people are not in a dark night. Although many might classify themselves as religious, they are far from the beginnings of a journey to God, and seem to use religious language for social or psychological support or for manipulation.

However, the situation created for normal citizens is so evil, oppressive, and hate-filled that it can cause a dark night for those who witness it, reflect on it, and confront it with

God's hope-filled plan for humanity. How does society experience such decay, when did it start, why is it there are so few servants of the people? Once again, instead of being forced to confront personal sinfulness, helplessness, and emptiness, we are immersed in social, organized sin on a scale that overwhelms us. Is there any way to get out of this?—probably not! Are there people, up-and-coming, who can challenge this and change it?—it seems unlikely! These people talk endlessly, presenting their arguments for why things are the way they are. No one believes these discursive justifications, and all see intuitively that they are wrong. We are in a societal dark night with no hope of getting out of it on our own. Here the notion of the dark night includes the social evils of our society that we see every day. John's poem, "one dark night," emerges from pain, torture, and neglect by the society of his day. Moreover, all John's efforts at renewal and reform implied a desire to change the social fabric of his day.[22] It seems everything we hoped human community could provide is diverted to a selfish few, and the majority is left empty. It is no use thinking about the way things used to be, or remembering former good times, or doing whatever little good we can. Rather, we need a transformation and renewal that can bring forth a new vision of society.[23] This will not come from the top-down, neither in society nor in the Church. It must percolate up from grass roots movements of those people who are pained by human sinfulness and offer themselves to the purifying interventions of God's dark, yet transforming nights.

Some contemporary obstacles to entering the dark night

A reduced ideal of the Christian calling.

The dark night is by invitation only! God invites and draws people through the dark nights to union, when God so desires. However, a person has to want it and to have prepared by virtue, prayer, and solid ascetical practices. John says there are all kinds of reasons why someone does not enter the dark night (A. Prologue.3-7). He points out that some may be satisfied with "moral and pleasing topics addressed to the kind of spiritual people who like to approach God along sweet and satisfying paths" (A. Prologue.8). Nowadays, we spend a lot of time dabbling in religious practices that have no chance of leading us to the union God offers.

John for his part offers us a challenge that is profound. For John the starting point is lower—in the negative views he presents of human sinfulness. John presents the spiritual journey as longer—with all its challenges. Finally, the point of arrival is much higher—when a person is transformed and divinized, while retaining his or her own humanity. John gives us space for liberty, fulfillment, and grace; it is a great and noble calling. However, we must strengthen our motivation by choosing to love Christ above all things and seeking the life God offers.

We must prophetically take a position against minimalistic approaches to spiritual development. We must set our goal on the mountain top—"perfect union with God through love." As John expected, people easily become satisfied with the little they have and with small desires, and this clinging to what easily satisfies blocks their readiness and willingness to move on. All around us we hear good dedicated people who have a reduced ideal of the Christian calling, and this is a contemporary obstacle to entering the dark night on the way to union.

A lost appreciation of the presence of God.

So much of contemporary life with its focus on consumerism or, within the Church, on ministerial action downplays the importance of simply being in the presence of God. Often there is little appreciation of that realm of life beyond this one that gives meaning to everything we do. We live unconnected to the God of our hopes. We forget that the slightest degree of loving union "is more than all the works you can perform" (S. 12; C. 29.2). Contemporary religion frequently presents us with a small God, rather than the image that enthralls and fills John with mystical enthusiasm (see C. 36.5 and 11.10). We, too, make God small when our prayer consists primarily in our one-sided requests and plans, without waiting and listening to God.

In stillness, inspiration, concentration, and silence we can re-train ourselves to recollection and to living in the presence of God in every moment of our lives. Finding God in all things means learning to see connections between daily events and the mystery of our awesome God. Listening, seeing, sitting still and doing nothing, breathing in rhythm with our hearts, relaxing, concentrating, worshiping the goodness of God, and recognizing God's purifying actions in our world, are all ways to increase our recollection and awareness of the presence of God. We must give time every day to savoring the presence of God

The destruction of the concept of love.

John's journey of love encounters problems in a world where love is often misunderstood. Love is reduced to sentiments, to narcissism, to the sublimation of sexual encounters, and to a falsifying of true mystical union. It is viewed even in spirituality as a soft journey rather than the robust journey of faith. Love is often seen as self-satisfying rather than generous self-gift. But John warned, "A soul that is hard because of self-love grows harder" (S. 30). In our contemporary world few so-called leaders see love as a solution to any problem. It is almost as if we are failing to train each other to love, or that parents are failing to train their children to love and no longer offer their home and family as schools of love.

In the passive dark nights God teaches us how to love, taking away former ways of loving and giving us new ways to love. "For where there is true love of God, love of self and of one's own things finds no entry" (N.2. 21.10). However, it is love that guides us through the nights, and faith is insufficient in this journey unless it begins and ends in loving self-gift. We actively contribute to this journey by preparing ourselves to love. So, aware of contemporary failures, we need to begin the process of purifying selfish love and moving from self-centeredness to other-centeredness and God-centered lives. This is initially an ascetical task, and we must give ourselves to it enthusiastically and thus remove any obstacle of false love that blocks entry into the nights.

A dulling of the human spirit.

Almost nothing in our society nourishes contemplative reflectiveness. We are bombarded with commercialized self-gratification at every turn. We give importance to utilitarian approaches to life, to a work ethic, and to a changed approach to filling up time where there is no opportunity for reflection. We even fill our religious encounters with activities, as if we mistrust our own inner spirit, and our prayer becomes superficial. Trying to learn passivity in a world that only values action is not easy. In many ways this world of ours is not a very supportive place to live in if you search for spiritual values. There often seems a general dulling of the human spirit with its accompanying inability to think of God.

If we are to live here in this world while always thinking of being elsewhere—ultimately with God, and we must, then we need to unblock our frozen spirits. This will include finding time to think, reflect, and appreciate the fullness of the present moment. It means savoring beauty in nature, music, art, and even good food and wine. It will value friendship, family, and relationships. When we encounter God, we will be thrilled, excited, enthusiastic, but we must foster these qualities in daily life. We need to have passion and excitement for something. All this will require a creative approach to leisure.

Living in pervasive fear

Nowadays we live in fear. It has become a universal, present day motivation in every area of life. Men and women today face fear in financial instability, job insecurity, housing availability and crises, and relationships. We face fear in aging, health-care options, security, and mortality. We are threatened by powers all around us, from uncaring organizations, selfish and greedy business practices, governmental policies, and Church dictates. Ours is a fearful world, whether fear of the future and our self-destruction in war or environmental degradation, or of our materialistic approaches to life that put things and organizations before people. We are oppressed by fear of abuse in its many perennial forms and in its new forms that people create for their own evil satisfaction. We recoil from death and the unknown. The fear we experience is understandable because we live in a world where violence is tolerated and viewed as an acceptable way of life. We cannot watch the TV or read the newspaper or surf the internet without being filled with fears of one kind or another. Unfortunately, this pervasive fear controls us, which of course is why evil people use it so deliberately and effectively. John said that the devil disturbs the soul with fears of all kind to impede a soul's progress (N.2. 23.4). Nowadays, the world we live in does this. But, fear casts out love, creates enemies where there are none, establishes false priorities, and dries up the yearnings for union. We need initial peace to enter the dark night, and this world's overwhelming fears prevent good people from striving for the values that would bring them peace.

A desire to avoid suffering.

Our world is anything but perfect, and we confront suffering all around us, much of it caused by human beings. Our world does not like to think about suffering, whether it is political, social, or personal. Rather, as soon as we face suffering we want to bring closure and move on. So much suffering is the result of our sinfulness, selfishness, and disordered attitudes that have become part of our culture. We rationalize, justify, and religiously explain suffering. But all this anaesthetizes us to suffering and helps us avoid facing up to it. When we move to the religious-spiritual dimension we just do not believe that suffering should be a part of our encounter with a compassionate and loving God, and if we find suffering in our spiritual lives it seems something is wrong. John thinks otherwise. "God values in you the inclination to dryness and suffering for love of him more than all the consolations, spiritual visions, and meditations you could possibly have" (S. 14).

Our Christian faith lives in hope in spite of the brokenness around us. We must live differently because of Jesus' suffering and because of our own. In the nights we experience God's transforming love in our lives and this implies a call to ongoing transformation of ourselves and of our world. It means confronting suffering. We need to accept the mystery of suffering in life, appreciating that God is different than what we think God ought to be. Love includes suffering. "The very fire of love that afterward is united with the soul, glorifying it, is what previously assailed it by purging it" (F. 1.19). Suffering is often linked to the problem of evil and cries out for redemptive love. Moreover, how we deal with suffering transforms us or dehumanizes us. But, suffering is connected to faith; it is a characteristic of a fallen world that we believe needs redemption, and Jesus teaches us that confronting suffering is faith's proof of hope and love.

Ignorance and a lack of education on religious issues.

One of the basic presuppositions we need to have in preparation for entering the dark night is that there is a close link between knowledge and love. The more we know someone the more reasons we have to love. Love without knowledge is generally superficial. The journey through the nights is one of knowledge permeated by love. So our search for renewal and spiritual enlightenment needs to be grounded in solid theology, spirituality, and scripture. Unfortunately, this is frequently not the case. Rather, solid spirituality strains to be heard above the din of ignorance. In some groups trivia and programmed spontaneity take the place of searching to know more about the God we love, and some wallow in their anti-intellectualism.

Quality prayer and spiritual development require regular nourishment, especially contact with the Word of God. The effort to become more knowledgeable and educated about religion, beliefs, and faith is all part of the active nights. We can gain foundational knowledge in study, reflection, and sharing in community. We can pray over our new knowledge. Assuredly, this will be corrected and refined in the passive nights, but this acquired love to know God will be a great preparation for a new level of conviction.

We must confront these and other contemporary obstacles to entering the dark night. John's perennial challenge is powerful and exciting. He never underestimates the difficulties, but urges us on to the fulfillment that awaits us in the union of love to which God calls us

CHAPTER EIGHT
TWENTY QUESTIONS FOR JOHN OF THE CROSS AND HIS BOOK THE DARK NIGHT

1. Is the dark night necessary for everyone?

John states clearly that unless God places a person in the dark night, he or she cannot purify self of all imperfections nor prepare for union (N.1. 3.3; 7.5). However, he also points out that not everyone moves on to the passive night of spirit (N.1. 14.5); it depends on God's sovereign will. John says it is God's desire to place people in the dark night so that they can move on to union, but for one reason or another they do not respond. Sometimes they do not want to enter; then again they may be without suitable spiritual directors to help them. "God gives many souls the talent and grace for advancing, and should they desire to make the effort they would arrive at this high state" (A. Prologue.3). At times God makes them advance without their help or cooperation, but then their progress is slow. Some go so far as to hinder God's efforts. What John does insist on is that purification is necessary for union with God. One who prepares himself or herself for entrance into the dark night takes a short cut to progress. Those who do not will need to face long times of gradual purification in this life and in the next before they are ready for union with God in love (A.1. 4.3).

We must always remember that John was an all-or-nothing kind of person. For him the only choice was todo or nada. His goal is very clear—union with God in love, the best of which a person is capable. To ask John whether we can get by with less would be outside his interests. Moreover, he begins his work with the transition from beginners to proficients, and we only know what he thinks of the development of the life of beginners from his many parentheses when he looks back to what things used to be like. He even suggests that the stage of beginners is permanent for some.

It is also important to point out that it is difficult to get through life without dealing with the passive night in the many experiences we must face. We know about John's evangelizing and educational ministries to those in need in regions around the monasteries where he lived and the help he gave them in spiritual direction. He treated these good people with respect, never despised how they were, and nourished them at whatever point in life they found themselves. His pastoral practice implied the dark night of spirit was not essential to individuals' journey to God. However, the purification that comes with the dark night is necessary in one way or another for union with God in love. God has created each of us with a longing that only God can satisfy and with a capacity for union with God. Until these yearnings are satisfied we will always be incomplete. This purification requires the dark night or something like it.

2. How did John relate to organized religion?

Organized religion today is dealing with a crisis of confidence as it faces scandals throughout the world. It is not unlike what John had to deal with. Then again, John not only had to deal with conflicting authorities, but elements in the Church tried over and over again to condemn some features of his work. Nevertheless, John gave himself to the reform within the legitimate Church structures of his day. Over and over again, he placed his writings before the Church's scrutiny, humbly accepting its authority (A. Prologue.2; C. Prologue.4).

Moreover, John saw his spiritual system as integrally related to the Church's sacramental economy (A.2. 22.7 and 11). He saw the Church as the normal channel through which God works, and anything unusual, such as miracles, is only out of necessity (A.3. 31.9). Thus, John directed his readers away from exceptional mystical graces and stressed the basic ecclesial plan of God (A.2. 24.3). While God reveals special knowledge in the nights, John can repeat, "I have told you all things in my Word, my Son and . . . I have no other word" (A.2. 22.5). In fact, even in the higher levels of mystical union, John returns to speak about the incarnation.

John understood the Church as God's channel of revelation, of authentic teaching and interpretation (A.2. 27.4; 29.12), and of religious practices (A.2. 22.7; A.3. 35.3; 42.6). His view was something like many contemporary people used to have before the Second Vatican Council. John did not have our contemporary ecclesiology of community, charisms, liturgy, and mutual responsibility.

3. How does John show appreciation for the uniqueness of women's journey?

We have 33 of John's letters, 20 of which were sent to nuns of the reform, including two for groups of nuns. Eight of the letters were sent to lay women. The *Spiritual Canticle* was dedicated to Mother Ann of Jesus, the prioress of Granada, while the *Living Flame*, both poem and commentary, were written for Doña Ana del Mercado y Peñalosa, whom John addresses as "very noble and devout lady." John clearly appreciates their correspondence and writes to some with evident friendship. He shares with them as equals, interested in the matters they raise, while also openly sharing some of his own trials with them. He is aware of their importance to the reform and sees them as foundations of the future renewal and growth. He shows genuine affection for them in their spiritual trials and respectfully challenges them in any weaknesses he sees. He treats all the women to whom he writes with respect, deals with many serious practical issues with a clear awareness of their competence, and speaks of the most profound spiritual matters with an acknowledgement of the recipients' advanced spiritual development. Were John to have shown the typical approach to women in his day it would not have been with such appreciation for their exceptional competence.

John shows no gender discrimination. In fact, he does not seem to distinguish between men and women when he writes, which would be unusual for his day. John treats them as equals, which needs to be considered a position of exceptional respect for women's roles in his day. Of course, John was formed and trained by one of the most stable and spiritually mature women of the age, Mother Teresa of Jesus, who showed several times she was in no mood to allow negative approaches to women. She told the provincial to send her women of intelligence and she would not worry at all as to whether they had dowries or not. She wanted the office in the vernacular so the nuns could understand it. She was accustomed to contacting the most influential people of the day, including Philip II. John had a good teacher.

4. Does one need a spiritual director?

John advises the need for a good spiritual director, and the prologue to the *Ascent* gives many references to difficulties of individuals striving on their own to pursue this journey. Nowadays we have to acknowledge that there are many situations where individuals are on their own. Since the point of departure for the spiritual journey is not one's own efforts but God who in love for us draws us to divine life, it would seem that it is sufficient to be open to God's grace. However, John insisted on the need of a spiritual director for the journey (see S. 5, 7, 8, 9, 11, 13). There is always the temptation to apply ideas or texts to oneself, but it is better with a spiritual guide. John speaks at length about spiritual directors, and not always positively. He clearly considers that some are ill-prepared and stunt a person's growth, blocking their entrance into the dark night (A. Prologue.3-5).

John wants individuals who journey through the nights to have a spiritual guide who is learned, discreet, and experienced (F. 3.30). The director should be learned in Scripture, spirituality, theology, and the spiritual classics. He or she should be discreet with ability to make prudent sound judgments with a discerning heart. He or she should have experience of spiritual direction, life and prayer. There are plenty of people who want to be spiritual directors for their own satisfaction. Then again, there are some who are "general practitioners," maybe qualified for the early stages of beginners and their meditation. John seeks directors who are capable of dealing with the complexities of the nights and also have the humility to appreciate that "they themselves are not the chief agent, guide, and mover of souls in this matter, but the principal guide is the Holy Spirit" (F. 3.46). So, John wants an individual to choose a spiritual director who has experience of the spiritual journey, knows his or her limitations, and is not attached to some neatly packaged method. The director is not a companion on the journey, for companions can both get lost. Rather, an individual should choose a guide who knows the way, understands its ups and downs, and has lots of compassion for what an individual is going through during this journey. John also insists that one take care in selecting a director, for better or worse he or she can end up very like the spiritual director (F. 3.30).

5. What is John's approach to created things?

John speaks positively about the beauty of nature (C. 14-15) and insists that a reconciled approach to God includes a renewed and transformed approach to creation. He sees the incarnation as relating to all creation, and the *Spiritual Canticle* and the *Dark Night* are powerfully positive regarding creation. He appreciates sculptures, created forms, architecture. He likes dance, music, and relationships with people. Even when John speaks about rejecting objects of sense, he is speaking about those that get in the way or replace God. He is seeking a total self-gift to God in which everything is integrated. The purpose of the dark night is not to deprive oneself of objects but to arrive at a lack of desire for them as ends in themselves. It is not created objects that get in the way, but addictive, unfree desire that controls choices about them.

The seeming negativity that appears at first sight is not towards creatures in themselves but is a negativity towards desire for created things that can lead away from God (A.1. 3.4). Again, we must be careful even here, for John's negative approach is not to desires in themselves, but to inordinate—habitual, voluntary, imperfect—desires for created things—be they material, spiritual, or religious. When John refers to inordinate desires he means desires for something other than God instead of God. Nada refers to anything that leads us away from God. Todo is everything in so far as it is integrated in our unified self-gift to God (see "Prayer of a soul taken with love"). When inordinate desires are controlled one can appreciate that all creation comes from "the hand of my Beloved" (C. v. 4; see also vs. 14-15).

6. How would John deal with the global issues or awareness of suffering in the world?

John lived in times very different than ours when we have instant communication and deal every day with what happens all over the world. However, John had a profound awareness of the global issues of his day and the extensiveness of human suffering. He lived at the time of Philip II when Spain was really the center of the political world, often fighting wars for wealth, imperialism, and pseudo-religious reasons. The military campaigns of the king throughout Europe were well known, since many in John's time were paying excessive taxes to finance the wars. The conflicts between Philip and the papacy would also be well known to John. So, he would have a good knowledge of European politics, not to mention awareness of Spain's expansion to the new world.

On a personal level John knew poverty, hunger, unemployment. He lived surrounded by greed and injustice. He lived through two periods of famine, "the barren years," and saw the consequences especially for the poor. He lived with racism in the south of the country, and with versions of the caste system that every country develops and even fosters. He also experienced persecution, inquisitional controls and interrogation, and the oppression by the elites of his day.

Thus, John knew well many of the global crises of his day. He experienced the consequences of greed for money and power and suffered from the corruption of the powerful of his time. John believed that evil is in the heart. The disorders that concerned him were not the failures or imperfections into which just people can sometimes fall. Rather, he concentrated on disorders that are profound misdirections of life that affect the affective core of our lives and value systems. Sometimes these disorders are difficult to discover because they are made to appear quite normal, justified as acceptable practice in a particular culture or time, rooted in the people's common life, and even religiously supported. When we see this kind of trend in a culture we are face to face with serious disorder. When this happens to a culture it destroys it from within. Thus, John sees the development of the spiritual life as intimately linked to more global issues. These latter can also hinder the development of one's spiritual life and need to be purified. For John, the loss of values within a culture impacts the spiritual development of all of us. The evils of our world, like those of his, must be challenged as part of the journey to love.

7. Does John frequently use Scripture?

John says that his primary help in explaining his teachings on the dark night will be Scripture, since "Taking Scripture as our guide we do not err," since the Holy Spirit speaks to us through Scripture. Moreover, in using Scripture John says he does not wish "to deviate from the true meaning of Sacred Scripture" (see A. Prologue.2). John quotes 684 times from the Old Testament and 376 times from the New Testament. He uses stories and images from Scripture throughout his writings. Each of his great poems contains an action word in the first verse—like an exodus theme. John uses stories from Scripture that are archetypes of our own stories. These stories are symbolic expressions of common human experiences (C. Prologue.1). John's frequent reference to the *Song of Songs* appears throughout his writings, and he has several other references to the Eucharist in his poems. So, John's use of Scripture is more as revealed symbols of our own life and calling. He does not have our contemporary literary critical approach to Scripture.

8. Is John dependent on other writers?

John was influenced by developments in the Carmelite Order before and after the reform. He read extensively the theology and piety of his day. His own writings were the result of a long preparation. Unlike Teresa, he did not think of publishing anything. Rather, like St. Paul in his letters, John writes to answer specific questions from real people. Thus, there is always someone behind the text, and this gives validity and immediacy to his work. He reflects on his own experiences and on other people's experiences too, and then he draws out insights to help others.

Besides his knowledge of Scripture, John was an outstanding theologian and much appreciated in his own day in Alcalá de Henares, Segovia, and Baeza. He had studied extensively and used the monastery libraries. However, he gives no references to books in his writing. Two of John's companions tell us that they saw John write but that he never used other books.

He mentions the ten steps of the ladder of love and says that St. Bernard and St. Thomas also deal with these steps (they actually come from a 14th century Dominican called Helvicus Teutonicus). Jean Baruzi, Damaso Alonso, and Fr. Crisogono have identified explicit quotes from other writers along with several comments that call to mind other writers, but all are indirect and not substantial. For all the major parts of John's work he is totally original.

9. Is John pessimistic?

Throughout the *Dark Night* John speaks of "the soul" and its journey to God, while frequently speaking negatively of all things material. However, when he speaks of the soul it is not some spiritual aspect of a human being but each of us as person in our totality. He is not making any distinction between spirit and matter, viewing the former as positive and the latter as negative. Rather, the soul is John's way of referring to every Christian in the ordinary circumstances of daily life.

Even John's use of sensual and spiritual is not to be viewed as static divisions of the human being but as dynamic views of human development (see A.1. 6.2). A person is either led by selfish values or by God-directed values. John speaks of the human condition more than human nature, and he describes that condition very negatively. However, he is not a pessimist, nor does he despise humanity. His descriptions may well be discouraging (see A.1. 6-10; A.3. 19; N.1. 2; N.2. 2), but actually reflect a spiritual realism. In relation to the call to union with God in love, the circumstances in which we often find ourselves are really bad. John describes individuals in relation to what ought to be.

At the start of the spiritual journey, even though one's situation is bad and unhealthy, a person is essentially good because created by God (A.1. 9.3). At the end of the journey when one is transformed, his or her essence remains fully human as before and not absorbed (A.2. 5.7). John sees an individual as always a person in need of transformation, and so he is always sensitive to each one's personal situation and subjective reactions. If someone finds sensible goods useful for delight in God and elevating self towards God, fine! Keep them for a while (A.3. 24.4). John is a man who hopes we will attain what we are capable of. If anything, he is an optimist; setting before us goals that few other writers think we are capable of attaining. We would do well to give up on more optimistic systems that simply do not work, and face the fact that John is more real and thorough than most other spiritual writers.

10. Is John's teaching only for religious and celibates?

John says it is his main intention (A. Prologue.9). However, we have seen how many laity were directees of John, and some of them were clearly well advanced in the spiritual life. Some were also married. While John naturally claims to be writing for the members of the reform he has no control over the ecclesial influence of his work. The *Dark Night* is not a reserved book for a spiritual elite, but "the soul" is easily understood as every human being who longs for deeper union with God. More people read the *Dark Night* today than ever and find its adult spirituality and strong love to be challenging.

John does not consider that a person has two parts, natural and supernatural, material and spiritual, sense and spirit, lower and higher. John is encouraging people to give the whole of their lives to God. So, for him, the usual distinctions between good and evil do not work in the same way. Any object—good as well as evil, can block one's progress. One can just as easily be attached to one's devotions or spiritual director as to money, or to seek self-satisfaction in prayer or in power. John wants us to integrate every aspect of life into our total gift to God.

We should also keep in mind the state of religious life when John wrote. Teresa called the monastery of the Incarnation "that Babylon," and many religious were in monasteries because their families could not find adequate dowries or property to find suitable marriages for them. John was dealing with people who were moving towards reform, good, dedicated individuals who were making a fundamental option for a God-directed life. Many laity, including married, find themselves in such circumstances today. There is nothing in John that requires celibacy for progress in the spiritual life. In fact, celibacy can become a spiritual good to which individuals and organizations become attached—an attachment that needs the purification of the passive night of spirit. John's teaching is readily available for all people who long to journey to union with God with the whole of their lives.

11. How does John's work measure up to modern psychology?

John uses scholastic psychology of his own time to explain a person's reactions to the sensory. His methods in spiritual direction show he has carefully observed people over many years. His work is a careful and reflective study of human development, and he presents us with a wealth of knowledge about human emotions, human fulfillment, and the search for one's authentic self.

Some scholars have focused on John's psychology, especially his approach to love. John Welch suggested the studies and insights of writers like Carl Jung, Bernard Lonergan, James Fowler, and Gabriel Moran illumine the spirituality of John and are themselves illumined by John's work.[24] According to Kevin Culligan, "St. John's understanding of human development, unconscious motivation, emotional healing, and interpersonal dynamics anticipates and is confirmed by modern psychology. In other words, even by today's standards, the saint could be seen as a scientific psychologist at work."[25]

12. Is John's poetry unique?

John's poetry shows influences from three Spanish poets, Garcilasco de la Vega, Juan Boscán, and Sabastián de Cordoba. John may well have read their work when he studied in Medina del Campo. Their influence included the meter John used and the pastoral themes they developed. It is also possible that John took the title of his great poem, "One Dark Night," from Garcilasco's "Second Ecologue," in which the lover, Albanio, leaves "in the silence of the dark night."[26] John was also very influenced by the *Song of Songs* and its central theme of the beloved in search of the lover which Christianity has interpreted as the disciple and Christ. In fact, John modifies four secular poems, transposing them to a religious level (a lo divino). Both Menendez Pelayo and Damaso Alonso claimed that John was the greatest poet of Spain. John uses poetry to express the ineffable in order to remind himself of the experience and to teach others of God's encounters with those who seek union. John uses the forms of the poetry to express spiritual insights. Thus, stanzas 1-12 of the *Spiritual Canticle* describe the anxious search for God. They contain no adjectives or adverbs in Spanish, but portray quick movement with no concern for details, only the longing to find one's lover as quickly as possible. These stanzas contrast with 13-21 which contain numerous adjectives and convey the broad, expressive fullness and satisfaction of encounter.

The *Living Flame* consists of four stanzas of six lines each—rather than the usual five—a poetic format unique to John. Again, he uses the longer form to convey his spiritual teachings. They are slower and richer, giving the impression of fullness and satisfaction. Where one would expect the stanzas to end (after line four), they go on for another two lines. Thus, he creates the dynamism of the abundant satisfaction of love. When John writes poetry it is not as a poet but as a mystic. The poems are the expression of his spiritual experience. Their uniqueness does not come from a skilful combination of words or from a refined imagination, but from exceptional inner transformation.

John's work is an extraordinary combination of the purity of his message, the human authenticity of his teaching, and his beautiful quality of expression. Since John's poems are not the result of creative writing and imaginative expression, but rather of depth experience and inner transformation, they are always alive and change as readers change. Their suggestive language means one thing this month and another next month, as readers identify with the inner transformation and feel the impact of God on their lives. John does not write his poems for others' entertainment and appreciation, he writes poetry to communicate, to re-live, and to facilitate in others the direct experience of spiritual encounter. When we read we find not only his story but our own as well.

13. What causes the passive nights?

The passive night of sense and the passive night of spirit are caused by God. The passive night of spirit includes infused contemplation and the passive night of sense may. The individual does nothing except receive, and God accomplishes what God intends (A.1. 13.1). In contemplation a person experiences God in a different way than previously. This experience is an experience of faith, and so John refers to the dark night of faith. In the passive night of sense God's interventions cause the end of discursive prayer and the beginning of an encounter with God through the simple act of contemplation. In the passive night of spirit a person experiences God in a radically different way than formerly, realizing that God can no longer be known by our previous experiences or categories. Instead of the intellect focusing on its natural object of knowledge, God purifies and illumines it by faith. We thus learn to "know" God more by faith than by the accumulation of knowledge about God. Likewise instead of the memory focusing on its usual object of past experiences or imagined futures, God transforms it so that it directs itself to an unknown future in hope in God. We thus can have confidence and rejoice more in the future God holds out to us than in remembering, accumulating or avoiding past experiences or anticipating futures we make up, limit, or try to control for ourselves. Then, instead of the will concentrating on the satisfactions it finds in many objects of desire, God purifies it to integrate all its longings on love of God alone and all things in God (see "Prayer of a soul taken with love").

There are indications that the individual contributes to this experience, even though a passive recipient—surrendering oneself to God is a deliberate act, as is focusing one's attention, keeping oneself empty. Moreover, as the passive nights throw further light on one's sinfulness, an individual responds by actively seeking to remove such failures.

Part of what causes the pain of the passive nights is that the new experience of God is an inflow of love. This love brings the pain of unworthiness, distress, and unfulfilled longings (N.1. 11). So, contemplation that causes the passive nights should not be understood simply as illumination, but also as the hidden, purifying effects of the enkindling of love.

The experience of the dark night is not the same for everyone who enters it. St. Teresa, St Therese and St. John of the Cross experience the night in differing ways. John tells us that the experience and intensity varies according to individuals and God's sovereign will. Even the resulting experiences are different—physically, psychologically, mentally, emotionally, and spiritually.

14. Is John's imagery unique?

An image is something that gives us a moment's intuition into a reality. Thus, national flags remind us of a country. At times an image evokes a particular affective or emotional response, and we call such sign-images symbols. Thus, one's own particular national flag may well evoke a feeling or sense of patriotism. When an image is symbolic one's perception is immediate, not before or after. So the symbol and response it evokes are indivisible.

Some symbols used by John are archetypes; water immediately suggests satisfying thirst and cleansing; fire evokes warmth and light; light implies illumination and guidance; night evokes darkness, fear, and even a sense of being lost. John uses all these images-symbols as do most spiritual writers. John's use for the most part is not unique. Now and again images-symbols are enriched by cultures and by religions. Thus, the Bible speaks of God guiding the Chosen People through the night with a pillar of fire. Elsewhere the Bible speaks of God's love and union with the Chosen People as a matrimony, and this is continued in the theme of the love and union between Christ and his Church. Again these and similar images are commonly found in spiritual writers.

John uses the image-symbol of matrimony to express total mutual gift, union and permanence of the relationship. Unlike other mystics, for example Hugh and Richard of St. Victor and St. Bernard, John does not use explicit sexual language in reference to conjugal union. However, there are clear passionate expressions of love and mutuality (F. 1; C.

verses 23, 24, 27, 34). His *Spiritual Canticle* is a powerful paralleling of the *Song of Songs* to anxious search, yearning for union, intimacy, and passionate love. For intimacy, tenderness, and passion, he also uses the relationships of mother-child or friends. So, John's use is a little different than some other writers, but matrimony remains an important image-symbol (see C. 22.3 and 6). It also should be pointed out that matrimony as a symbol of mystical union presumes an old view of matrimony that implies a passivity on the part of the woman.

John's unique contribution to the use of images-symbols in spiritual theology is his use of the image-symbol of the dark night, which he uses 247 times. Other writers use this but it is John who has given this image-symbol both its originality and its depth of meaning. This image-symbol naturally evokes darkness, uncertainty, anxiety, and even fear. Religion has enriched this with the ideas of God's presence and guidance. John's own experiences in Castile, especially Medina del Campo and Segovia, and above all in the prison in Toledo, all enriched this concept. For John, "night" takes on a meaning for the whole of life (A.1. 3.4), and most particularly it describes the whole spiritual journey. John shows the movement from "dark night," "glad night," "guiding night," "night more lovely than the dawn," "night that has united the Lover with his beloved" ("Dark Night," vs 1, 3, 5), "the tranquil night at the time of the rising dawn," "the serene night, with a flame that is consuming and painless" (C. vs. 14, 39).

15. Is everyone called to contemplation?

John describes the dark night in more detail in the *Dark Night* than in the *Ascent*. He calls contemplation infused even though he says it is still a beginning. John suggests that God does not bring everyone to contemplation (N.1. 9.9), but he seems to be referring to human weaknesses in entering the dark night as well as the sovereign wisdom of God for each person's good. Even many of those who give themselves to the life of the Spirit do not move on to contemplation. When John wonders why, he answers "God knows best."

So, like the dark nights, contemplation is not necessary for salvation but it is necessary to attain in this life the goal of union with God in love, for it passively controls anything that blocks this goal (N. Explanation.2). The first phase of infused recollection and beginning contemplation—namely that experienced by beginners as they move to being proficient in the spiritual life—happens to many people. The second phase—that which purifies the spirit and prepares it for union with God through love occurs for only a few on their journey from proficients to the deeper union.

While contemplation is a gift, we can prepare for it. Centering prayer is a method that helps one prepare for contemplation, whereas contemplation is passively received, a gift of God's Holy Spirit. For John, contemplation facilitates the purification of faith, hope, and love in preparation for union with God. Contemplation is God's invitation to welcome the divine love in our hearts. To do this we must let God first empty us so that we can be filled.

16. Is John's system of spiritual development the only one?

There are many different ways to God and different schools of spirituality have systematized their own approaches. These various systems contain several common features, often linked to the three-fold division of the spiritual journey into beginners, proficients, and perfect, corresponding to the purgative, illuminative, and unitive phases of life. Not all approaches are equally valid and some cease to be useful with the passage of time. In fact, nowadays many people work hard but get nowhere and instead of changing or looking for a more complete spirituality of breadth and depth, they continue with their same efforts and spiritual ideals. "Some people—and it is sad to see them—

work and tire themselves greatly, and yet go backward; they look for progress in what brings no progress and instead hinders them" (A. Prologue.7). At times it is important to state honestly that one's system of sanctification simply does not work. Prudent people would change and look for more wisdom elsewhere.

John's approach is simple, as he frees us from complicated spiritual structures and presents us with the human and Christian roots of profound religious experience. If not well understood and interpreted, he can seem harsh at times, but his approach has a ring of truth to it. He has personally made the journey, sees its internal logic, and places our own journey within the total plan of salvation. There is no rigidity in John's approach. Rather he has a fluidity and dynamism which respects each individual in his or her journey to God. John's approach is not the only one, but it is the straight and narrow one that leads to the summit of Mount Carmel.

17. How does John relate to the Gospel's emphasis on the resurrection?

Very well indeed! The dark night parallels the passion and leads to newness of life in the resurrection to union in love. John calls Jesus' passion "the death of love" (L. 11), and it prepares us for the resurrected life of union. "It is fitting that the soul be in this sepulcher of dark death in order that it attain the spiritual resurrection for which it hopes" (N.2. 6.1). John asserts that any evil tendency that needs to be uprooted "impedes the inner resurrection of the Spirit who dwells within" (L. 7). Not only do individuals enjoy this resurrection following purification, but so too does the whole world, and so John speaks of "this elevation of all things. . . through the glory of his resurrection" (C. 5.4).

John insists that there is no easy way to mystical union; it is a journey that goes through the passion. For each of us our own daily living of the passion consists in our journey through the dark nights. John lived at a time when the passion of the Lord was the primary focus in piety, but he leads us beyond the suffering to what follows in newness of life. Few have been so practical in indicating just what the passion really means for us, and few have been so clear in describing how wonderful the resurrection can be as John does in the *Living Flame*.

18. How do John's various works connect together?

Our return journey to God is modeled on God's journey to us which John describes in the "Romances." This is the point of departure for a full picture of John's works. The "Romances" describe how God's inner life is love and how God always deals with the world in love. Our return journey will always be some form of the beloved seeking out the Lover. John describes our journey to God in his four great works. The *Spiritual Canticle* and the *Living Flame of Love* describe the journey as a journey of love, whereas the *Ascent* and the *Dark Night* describe the journey from the perspective of faith. These are not two separate journeys but one integrated journey of love-filled faith or faith-filled love.

The *Ascent* deals with the journey in two stages which John calls dark nights, the active night of sense and the active night of spirit. The *Ascent* focuses more on our efforts during the journey and even deals with the stage of the beginners more than any of the other works, especially in its many parentheses. The *Dark Night* deals primarily with the latter stages of purification in its presentation of the passive night of sense and the passive night of spirit. This is some of the most difficult material that John presents. Both the *Ascent* and the *Dark Night* refer to the rewards of the journey in the union of love. The *Spiritual Canticle* deals with the whole of the journey from the perspective of love. However, it too deals with elements in the purification of the nights (see C. 1-12). All these three works are developmental, and each one covers much of the journey but from different perspectives. The

Living Flame describes the final stage of the spiritual journey. It is not developmental like the others, but it does have three retrospective sections that look back to the nights. Rather than progressive, the *Living Flame* looks at the final stage of the spiritual life from four points of view: the involvement of the Holy Spirit, the life-giving influence of the Trinity, the attributes of the Trinity revealed vitally, and communion with the Word of God.

So, each of these four works has many connections with the other three. These four major works, preceded by the "Romances," give us the complete system of John. His other works are moments of intuition, revealing insights into one or other aspect of the system, or as in the case of some of his shorter poems the whole system seen in brief.

19. Do we have any original copies of the *Dark Night*?

No, we do not. However, we have more copies of this work than of any other one written by John. Unfortunately, none of them is viewed as a copy of the original. The most critically accepted one is in the National Library of Madrid and is referred to as *Hispalense.*

20. Poverty, emptiness, nakedness, denial, and mortification—what would all this mean today?

Each of these words has a static meaning in everyday English. However, for John each one is dynamic. They each refer to the process of constantly becoming poorer, constantly emptying oneself of false values, and so on. They are not negative attitudes but expressions of a positive orientation, namely to always give preference to everything that is of God. It is unfortunate that with these words we often think of mortification as "putting to death" certain aspects of ourselves. This is not so. We have seen often enough that John is firm in his desire that all of one's life be reborn in the journey to God. So all these attitudes form part of an ongoing re-education of the will as love and motivating energy to always choose whatever is conducive to a God-directed life. We do not tend to view these matters as either/or choices. Rather, since the Second Vatican Council defined the autonomy of earthly realities and their intrinsic goodness, we tend to seek always to integrate everything we do into our total commitment to God. There are not some aspects of our life that are better than others. All can be directed to God. So, the contemporary effort we must all engage in is the commitment to integrate all our life in one total self-gift to God.

NOTES

1. John returned to the rule as it was before the mitigations. The original primitive rule was given to the monks on Mount Carmel by Albert, Patriarch of Jerusalem.

2. See Leonard Doohan (*The Contemporary Challenge of John of the Cross*, Washington, DC: ICS Publications, 1995), pp. 20-22.

3. Elizabeth Hamilton, *The Life of St Teresa of Avila*, (New York, Charles Scribner's Sons, 1959), p. 65.

4. John also mentions two nights of sense and spirit and indicates that each is both active and passive, thus giving a total of four nights. However, these are all parts of the one purifying night.

5. John describes the development from beginners to proficients in N.1. 8.

6. The *Ascent* ends without discussion of the other three passions or of directive and perfective spiritual goods (see A.3. 35 where John establishes the divisions that he does not complete).

7. It is worth recalling a comment by Fr. Crisogono de Jesus Sacramentado, *The Life of St. John of the Cross* (New York: Harper and Brothers, 1958), pp. 222-3. "His major works, then, were a gradual development. They were preceded by small fragments which developed into chapters. It should be remarked, however, that these first writings already have a definite character about them when the author gave shape to the greatest of his works—the *Ascent of Mount Carmel*—they were to pass into it textually, without emendation or redrafting. It can be seen that his system was already mature."

8. Seeing life in these categories can be helpful but there is generally overlap. The passive night of sense can be from the beginning provided an individual is open to receive and understand the challenges. Then again, there is a way in which the active night of spirit is also connected to sense in that it is about gratification concerning spiritual things of intellect, memory, and will that spills over into the senses. Furthermore,

194 Leonard Doohan

the passive night of sense can be about unconscious sins, attitudes, and gratifications that are discovered through contemplation.

9. Jean Baruzi, *Saint Jean de la Croix et le Probleme de l'Experience Mystique* (Paris: Libraire Felix Alcan, 1924) makes an interesting comment: "For John of the Cross, the rules of mortification are mystical rather than ascetical."

10. ". . . [T]he soul must be led to a life of perfect abnegation and profound and continuous recollection, which will maintain it wholly beneath the hand of God, at His disposal to be taught and trained by Him. Such is the work of the active purification of Spirit." Gabriel of St. Mary Magdalen, *St. John of the Cross: Doctor of Divine Love and Contemplation*, (Westminster, MD: Newman Press, 1951), 32.

11. Charles Peguy, *God Speaks* (New York: Pantheon, 1945).

12. This section is dependent on Fr. Steven Payne's article, "To Ask God the Right Questions," *Spiritual Life* 25 (1979): 204-214.

13. Payne, "To Ask God the Right Questions," p. 209.

14. Payne, "To Ask God the Right Questions," p. 211.

15. See Patrick Berquist, "A Long Dark Winter's Night," *Spiritual Life* 53 (2007): 35-40.

16. See William Quinn, "Beyond the Signs of the Times: Priesthood and Religious Life in a Troubled Season," *Spiritual Life* 37 (1991): 101-106.

17. Patrick J. McDonald and Claudette McDonald, "Dark Nights and Hard Days: A View of Marital Spirituality," *Spiritual Life* 39 (1993): 150-159.

18. These stages are taken from the article by Patrick J. McDonald and Claudette McDonald, "Dark Nights and Hard Days: A View of Marital Spirituality," *Spiritual Life* 39 (1993): 150-159.

19. McDonald, p. 544.

20. McDonald, p. 155.

21. Mary Frohlich, "John's 'One Dark Night': Romantic, Political or Mystical," *Spiritual Life* 37 (1991): 41. See the whole article, pp. 38-47.

22. See Frohlich, "John's 'One Dark Night': Romantic, Political or Mystical," pp. 44-45.

23. See Sr. Constance FitzGerald, "Impasse and Dark Night," in *Living With Apocalypse*, Spiritual Resources for Social Compassion (San Francisco: Harper and Row, 1984), 410-433, especially "Societal Impasse," pp. 422-425.

24. See John Welch, *When Gods Die: An Introduction to John of the Cross* (New York: Paulist Press, 1990), 2.

25. See Kevin G. Culligan, *Towards A Model of Spiritual Direction Based on the Writings of St. John of the Cross and Carl R. Rogers* (Ann Arbor: MI: University Microfilms, 1981), .5.

26. See Gerald Brenan, *St. John of the Cross: His Life and Poetry* (England: Cambridge University Press, 1973), 125.

BIBLIOGRAPHY

Baruzi, Jean. *Saint Jean de la Croix et le Probleme de l'Experience Mystique*. Paris: Libraire Felix Alcan, 1924.

Berquist, Patrick. "A Long Dark Winter's Night." *Spiritual Life* 53 (2007): 35-40.

Crisogono de Jesus Sacramentado,. *The Life of St. John of the Cross.* New York: Harper and Brothers, 1958.

Doohan, Leonard. *The Contemporary Challenge of John of the Cross*. Washington, DC: ICS Publications, 1995.

FitzGerald, Sr. Constance. "Living With Apocalypse." *Spiritual Resources for Social Compassion*. San Francisco: Harper and Row, 1984.

Frohlich, Mary. "John's 'One Dark Night': Romantic, Political or Mystical." *Spiritual Life* 37 (1991): 38-47.

Gabriel of St. Mary Magdalen. *St. John of the Cross: Doctor of Divine Love and Contemplation.* Westminster, MD: Newman Press, 1951.

Hamilton, Elizabeth. *The Life of St Teresa of Avila.* New York, Charles Scribner's Sons, 1959.

Kavanaugh, Kieran and Otilio Rodriguez. The Collected Works of St. John of the Cross. Washington, DC: ICS Publications, 1991.

McDonald, Patrick J. and Claudette McDonald, "Dark Nights and Hard Days: A View of Marital Spirituality." *Spiritual Life* 39 (1993): 150-159.

Payne, Steven. "To Ask God the Right Questions." *Spiritual Life* 25 (1979): 204-214.

Peguy, Charles. *God Speaks.* New York: Pantheon, 1945.

Quinn, William. "Beyond the Signs of the Times: Priesthood and Religious Life in a Troubled Season." *Spiritual Life* 37 (1991): 101-106.

Ruiz Salvador, Federico and others. *God Speaks in the Night.* Washington DC: ICS Publications, 191.

BOOKS AND E-BOOKS

THE CONTEMPORARY CHALLENGE OF JOHN OF THE CROSS
STUDIES OF THE MAJOR WORKS OF JOHN OF THE CROSS

This series presents introductions to each of the great works of John of the Cross. Each volume is a study guide to one of John's major works and gives all the necessary background for anyone who wishes to approach this great spiritual writer with appropriate preparation in order to reap the benefits of one of the most challenging figures in the history of spirituality. Each book is a complete introduction offering background, history, knowledge, insight, and theological and spiritual analysis for anyone who wishes to immerse himself or herself into the spiritual vision of John of the Cross.

While targeted to the general reader these volumes would be helpful to anyone who is interested in the spiritual guidance of this saint. These books give insight into the critical components of spiritual life and can be helpful for anyone interested in his or her own spiritual journey. They could be helpful for the many people involved in the spiritual guidance of others, whether in spiritual direction, retreat work, chaplaincy, and other such ministries. Throughout these books the reader is encouraged to develop the necessary attitudes, enthusiasm, spiritual sensitivity, and contemplative spirit needed to benefit from these spiritual masterpieces of John of the Cross. Attentive reflection on these studies will encourage readers to have a genuine love for John of the Cross and his approach to the spiritual journey.

These books give historical, regional, and religious background rarely found in other introductory books on John of the Cross. They each present an abbreviated and accessible form of John's great works. Later chapters in each book give John's theological and spiritual insights that could be used for personal reflection and group discussion. Sections abound in quotes and references from John's books and each sub-section can be used as the basis for daily meditation. The volumes complement each other, and together give the reader excellent foundation for reading the works of this great spiritual leader and saint.

Volume 1. John of the Cross: Your spiritual guide

This unique book is written as if John of the Cross is speaking directly to the reader. It is a presentation by John of the Cross of seven sessions to a reader who has expressed interest in John's life and teachings. This book introduces the great mystic and his teachings to his reader and to all individuals who yearn for a deeper commitment in their spiritual lives and consider that John could be the person who can guide them.

Table of contents
1. John's life as a contemporary life
2. John as a spiritual guide
3. John's vision of the spiritual life
4. Preparations for the spiritual journey
5. Major moments and decisions in the spiritual life
6. Necessary attitudes during the spiritual journey
7. Celebrating the goal of the spiritual journey

Volume 2. The Dark Night is Our Only Light: A study of the book of the *Dark Night* by John of the Cross

This introduction to the *Dark Night of the Soul* by John of the Cross gives all the necessary background for anyone who wishes to approach this great spiritual work with appropriate preparation in order to reap the benefits of one of the most challenging works in the history of spirituality. The book starts with the life of John of the Cross, identifying the dark nights of his own life. It provides the needed historical, religious, and personal background to appreciate and locate its content. It then presents readers with aids they can use to understand the work. With these preparations in mind the book moves on to present the stages of the spiritual life and the importance of the nights. A summary of John's own work brings readers in direct contact with the challenges of the message and its application today. The book ends with 20 key questions that often arise when someone reads this book.

Table of contents

Volume 3. The Spiritual Canticle: The encounter of two lovers. An introduction to the book of the *Spiritual Canticle* by John of the Cross

The book starts with the life of John of the Cross, showing how he was always a model of love in his own life, and how, guided by his own experience he became a teacher and later a poet of human and divine love. The book provides the needed historical, religious, and personal background to appreciate and locate its content. The book then presents the links between John's *Spiritual Canticle* and Scripture's love poem, the *Song of Songs*. A summary of John's own work brings readers in direct contact with the challenges of the message and its application today. With these preparations in mind the book moves on to present the stages of the spiritual life and the importance of the journey of love. The book then focuses on key concepts in the *Spiritual Canticle*, applying each of them to contemporary situations. Finally it considers the images of God presented in the book and how they relate to the spiritual journey.

Table of contents

Volume 4. The Living Flame of Love

The *Living Flame of Love* is the final chapter in John's vision of love. It describes the end of a journey that began in longings of love that became an experience of purification for the person seeking union. *The Living Flame of Love* picks up from the final stage of union in the love of spiritual marriage and describes, in great beauty, several aspects of this final stage in the union of love. All these ideas are part of John's wonderful vision of love. Many writers have emphasized the spiritual value of a life of love, but John's vision is more expansive and integrated than approaches presented by anyone else.

Table of contents

ALL BOOKS ARE AVAILABLE FROM AMAZON.COM

A Year with St. John of the Cross: 365 Daily Readings and Reflections

This book, *A Year with St. John of the Cross*, offers 365 daily readings and reflection. In this year with St. John of the Cross we will read and reflect on his life, ministry, spiritual direction, spirituality, as well as selections from all his works, short and long. The readings and reflections in this book will introduce readers to all these, as well as comments from many leading writers and commentators on John. This year will be an opportunity for readers to immerse themselves in the spirituality of John of the Cross. Each day offers a focused reading, four key reflections, and three specific challenges for the day.

For those who are enthusiastic supporters of St. John of the Cross, and for others who wish to discover new and substantial paths in their spiritual journey, this book is a one-of-a-kind opportunity to encounter John and his challenges like never before. Let your reading of this new book be your personal journey with John of the Cross, to a deeper union with God. One of the main uses of the book is to help readers who do not have ready access to a spiritual director. Maybe these readings and reflections will help. I hope you will find this special book helpful in your spiritual journey.

"Thank you so much for the excellent work. Your insights and reflection questions are wonderful."
"The clarity of the book, along with its depth without being complex, makes this work a real treasure."
"What a great idea and a superb execution, a work that will be helpful to so many."
"I recently purchased the Kindle edition of your book on St. John of the Cross. I have been reading from it each day as part of my prayer time. To sum it up in a word: wow!"

THE CONTEMPORARY CHALLENGE OF ST. TERESA OF AVILA

An Introduction to her life and teachings

This book is an introduction to the life and teachings of St. Teresa of Avila. It is a collection of notes and reflections taken from material I have presented in courses and workshops on St. Teresa over many years and in many countries to people from all walks of life who see Teresa's teachings on prayer as the vision and guidance they long for. This book on *The Contemporary Challenge of Saint Teresa of Avila*, is an introduction to her life and writings, and readers should use it as a companion to the careful and prayerful reading of Teresa's own writings. It is in no way a substitute for reading her works, in fact I have rarely quoted from her writings, insisting that readers must encounter them for themselves. I hope these notes and reflections will introduce readers to this giant in the history of spirituality and one of the greatest teachers of prayer that the world has ever known. This book is a companion to an earlier book, *The Contemporary Challenge of St. John of the Cross,* which was used extensively by individuals and groups as an introduction to St. John of the Cross' life and teachings. It was also used by many in formation programs. This current book on Teresa may well fulfill similar goals.

SPIRITUAL LEADERSHIP BOOKS

How to Become a Great Spiritual Leader: Ten Steps and a Hundred Suggestions

This is a book for daily meditation. It has a single focus—how to become a great spiritual leader. It is a book on the spirituality of a leader's personal life. It presumes that leadership is a vocation, and that it results from an inner transformation. The book proposes ten steps that individuals can take to enable this process of transformation, and a hundred suggestions to make this transformation real and lasting. It is a unique book in the literature on leadership.

This book is the third in a series on leadership. The first, *Spiritual Leadership: The Quest for Integrity* gave the foundations of leadership today. The second, *Courageous Hope: The Call of Leadership*, gave the contemporary characteristics and qualities of leadership. This third book focuses on the spirituality of the leader.

Courageous Hope: The Call of Leadership

This book's focus on leadership and hope is very appropriate given today's climate of distrust that many find results in a sense of hopelessness in their current leaders. Individuals and organizations are desperate for leaders of hope. Many books on leadership point to the need for inner motivation, but that inner motivation must be hope in new possibilities for a changed future. It is hope that gives a meaningful expression to leadership and enables the leader to be creative in dealing with the present. More than anything else it is a vision of hope that can excite and empower leaders to inspire others to strive for a common vision.

"Doohan strengthens our resolve. He restores our hope. And in an echo of Robert Frost, he is not only a teacher, but an awakener. May this book find you in a place where your will to grow is matched by an inner radiance to serve and help heal those around you... the reading will meet you there and the end result will be a gift to the world." **Shann Ray Ferch, PhD., MFA** Professor and Chair,

Doctoral Program in Leadership Studies, Gonzaga University. Editor, International Journal of Servant Leadership.

"Read every word of this book. Leaders stuck in the past, afraid to face the future, afraid to take a risk because they might be wrong need an infusion of Courageous Hope. People are not looking for a simple, blind-faith hope. They are looking for leaders with a deeper understanding of hope as described in this book." **Mary McFarland, PhD.,** Professor, and Former Dean of undergraduate through doctoral programs in Leadership. International consultant in leadership and education.

ANOTHER BOOK OF INTEREST

The One Thing Necessary: The Transforming Power of Christian Love.

This radical new interpretation of love as the touchstone of the Christian message, explores the human longing for meaning; the Scriptures; the relational model of the Trinity: the ideas of human vocation, destiny and community; the mystical spiritual traditions; and his own experiences to explain what love is, how we find it, and how it can change the world. Each of the seven chapters contains several quotes and focus points at the beginning and provocative questions at the end for reflection or discussion by adult religious educations and bible study groups.

"This book is all about love—and love as the one thing necessary. It is most certainly not about easy love or cheap grace. It is about the transforming power of Christian love. It is not only challenging but disturbing, a book written with conviction and passion." **Fr. Wilfrid Harrington, OP.,** Biblical scholar.

"[Doohan's] artful gathering and arranging of ideas reminds one of the impact of a gigantic bouquet of mixed flowers chosen individually and with great care." **Carol Blank**, Top 1000 reviewers, USA.

"Would that we heard more about this in our churches and religious discussions because, "this transforming power of Christian love will save the world" (p. 93). **Mary S. Sheridan**, "Spirit and Life."

The One Thing Necessary: The Transforming Power of Christian Love is available from www.actapublications.com and from amazon.com

ALL BOOKS ARE AVAILABLE FROM AMAZON.COM

Readers interested in John of the Cross can participate in the author's blog at
johnofthecrosstoday.wordpress.com

Visit the author's webpage at
leonarddoohan.com

www.ingramcontent.com/pod-product-compliance
Lightning Source LLC
LaVergne TN
LVHW051508080426
835509LV00017B/1975